MOTHER WAS A *Stranger*

Mary Green's Story, As Told By Her Eldest Daughter

JULIE LEEK

Author's Tranquility Press
ATLANTA, GEORGIA

Copyright © 2024 by Julie Leek

All rights reserved. No part of this publication may be reproduced, distributed or transmitted in any form or by any means, including photocopying, recording, or other electronic or mechanical methods, without the prior written permission of the publisher, except in the case of brief quotations embodied in critical reviews and certain other noncommercial uses permitted by copyright law. For permission requests, write to the publisher, addressed "Attention: Permissions Coordinator," at the address below.

Julie Leek/Author's Tranquility Press
3900 N Commerce Dr. Suite 300 #1255
Atlanta, GA 30344
www.authorstranquilitypress.com

Ordering Information:
Quantity sales. Special discounts are available on quantity purchases by corporations, associations, and others. For details, contact the "Special Sales Department" at the address above.

Mother Was A Stranger:
Mary Green's Story, As Told By Her Eldest Daughter / Julie Leek
Library of Congress Control Number: 2024921298
Hardback: 978-1-964037-82-0
Paperback: 978-1-964037-54-7
eBook: 978-1-964037-55-4

CONTENTS

CHAPTER 1 The Letter 1

CHAPTER 2 Memories 6

CHAPTER 3 A visit to meet Aunt Joan 16

CHAPTER 4 Aunt Dorothy 26

CHAPTER 5 Sad News 34

CHAPTER 6 The Children's Homes, Beeston 46

CHAPTER 7 The Children Remember 56

CHAPTER 8 Brick Walls 70

CHAPTER 9 A Will but No Way 77

CHAPTER 10 A Breakthrough 85

CHAPTER 11 Mother Was a Stranger 94

CHAPTER 12 The Freemans 103

CHAPTER 13 Before the Family Court Judge 111

CHAPTER 14 Rage, Rage Against the Dying
of the Light 122

CHAPTER 15 The Trail Goes Cold 135

CHAPTER 16 Fifteen Years Later 143

This book is dedicated to
my youngest sister Denise—
a belated blessing.

Gladys Mary Green (1931–1985)

MARY'S PARENTS:

Walter Edwin Green and Olive Minnie Poole

MARY'S SIBLINGS:

Caroline Joan Green (DOB: 1925)
Dorothy Olive Green (DOB: 1926)
John Edwin Green (DOB: 1927)

MARY'S ADOPTIVE PARENTS:

William Arthur Freeman and Lilian May Thursby adopted Mary in 1945 when she was thirteen years of age and changed her name to Lilian Audrey Freeman.

MARY'S HUSBANDS:

Mary, now called Audrey, married Thomas Roy Wolsey Schoolar in 1951. They separated in 1959 and later divorced. Mary married Herbert Goodwin in 1972.

MARY'S DAUGHTERS:

Mary had three daughters: Julie born in 1954, Jill born in 1956, and Denise born in 1964.

CHAPTER 1
The Letter

THE LETTER WAS LYING ON the mat when we arrived home. The postman rarely delivers before we leave for work, so any mail has to wait until we return in the evening to receive attention.

I am always disappointed when there is no mail. Letters have been an important part of my life. I can remember, in the first year at Margaret Glen-Bott Comprehensive School in 1965, being set up with an American pen pal, Cathy. We corresponded for a year or two, exchanging photos and adolescent chitchat, discussing personal likes and dislikes. Our enthusiasm gradually waned. Letters arrived less frequently, were shorter, slightly indifferent, until one of us sent the last letter and a reply was never forthcoming. Oh, but the excitement I felt at eleven years old when I received her first letter! Could I hear Big Ben chime from where I lived in Nottingham? Her friends thought the clothes I was wearing in the photo I sent were really "groovy." What was Nottingham like? How many department stores were there downtown? She had visited New York, and it was "huge and exciting"!

What must she have thought when I replied that there were only two major department stores in Nottingham? Of course, in my limited experience as an eleven-year-old shopper there were only two: Woolworths and the Co-op. My grandmother, who I lived with, only made infrequent bus trips to the city when she had an appointment with the chiropodist. I went more frequently with a couple of friends, but we had very little money to spend and would just wander round aimlessly, looking but without the means to buy anything, and usually we frequented these two department stores. My American pen pal obviously had the impression that England was a very small country if she thought that residents of Nottingham might be able to hear the chimes of Big Ben, and I'm afraid I did nothing to alter this opinion with my modest description of Nottingham city centre.

Then there was the letter Steve had written in reply to the six that I sent him. I was staying with an aunt and uncle in Wolverhampton for a week. We had been going out for a couple of months and saw each other most days. This was the first time we had been apart, and every day I spent an hour or two writing to him, although goodness knows what there was to write about! Toward the end of my stay, a letter arrived in response. It was written in capital letters, littered with spelling mistakes, and badly punctuated. Yet I knew that for Steve, hopelessly dyslexic and having completed his basic school education in the mid-sixties, before this condition was recognized or accommodated, these couple of pages represented more effort than I had put into all six of my letters. We have been married for over forty years now.

The letters my dad wrote in the late seventies meant a lot to me. Having visited friends in Eire (Southern Ireland) in 1978, we came back from our holiday to announce to our relatives that we would be going back in three weeks' time to live there with our six-year-old daughter, Emma.

I was surprised and pleased to receive regular letters from my dad. Since he remarried when I was seven years old, I had always felt his second family came first. My stepmother Eileen viewed me as a rival, and although Dad told me that I would be going to live with them after a few months when they had adjusted to married life, it never happened and I continued to live with his mother and father, my grandparents. It was therefore great to have the one-to-one attention that corresponding with him afforded me.

His last letter arrived in autumn 1980. He enclosed a cheque and asked that we use the money to come over from Ireland to attend his funeral.

The doctors had told him that despite the operation to remove a growth in his esophagus, tests showed the cancer had spread and there was nothing more they could do for him. It was just a matter of time. I spent a lot of hours over the next couple of days writing a reply, trying to say all the things I wanted to say and soon wouldn't be able to. I was comforted to know he received and read it before dying later the same day. He was forty-nine years of age.

Happy times in Arklow, Co. Wicklow (1978–1983)

In 1982, whilst still living in Arklow, Co. Wicklow, I received a letter from someone who was a stranger to me. It began, "You don't know me but…" I was fully halfway through reading it before the realization of who it was from hit me like a bolt of lightning. This letter was from Jill, my adopted sister.

My gran had told me about her in her own way when I was seven or eight years old.

"It's Jill's birthday today."

"Who's Jill?"

"Didn't you know you have a sister?"

"No."

"Yes, you have a sister two years younger than you. She had to be adopted because your mother was so ill. She couldn't cope. Well, it's her birthday today."

"Oh…"

Of course, I thought about her now and again over the years. Would I ever meet her? What was she like? She must live miles away in another part of the country. It turned out that Jill had been adopted by a couple who lived less than ten miles away in Gedling.

They had previously adopted another girl, Rosemary, so Jill had grown up with a sister. Her adoptive parents had always been open with her and had told her that her father's name was Schoolar and that she had a sister called Julie. Her mother had drawn the notice about our father's death in the local newspaper to her attention, and Jill resolved to contact me. Looking in the telephone directory, as she had many times before but never had the courage to dial any of the numbers, there were only four Schoolars listed. She dialed each in turn, pretending to be an old school friend who was searching for Julie Schoolar.

The second number she dialed put her in contact with my recently widowed stepmother, Eileen. Jill could not keep the pretense up for long as it soon became apparent that she did not even know the school I had attended, let alone been a "best mate"! She confessed that her real motive in trying to locate me was because she thought we were sisters. Eileen, fully aware of Roy's second daughter and that she had been adopted, asked point blank, "Are you Jill?"

Eileen gave Jill my address in Eire, hence the letter. We have been in touch with each other for more than thirty years now.

It has become quite unusual for me, and I suspect most others, to receive a real letter nowadays. By "real" I mean one that isn't a bill, a statement, or worse still "junk mail." One which isn't typed, isn't mass produced. Even in my current job as a secretary/ administrator, I rarely type letters now. Emails have caught on in a big way, and it is so convenient to dash one off, no need for the old protocols. Is it "Yours sincerely" or "Yours faithfully"? No need to worry now! Email terminology is much less formal, more relaxed, and yet far quicker and more efficient than "snail mail." Who wants a pen pal now? This is the IT generation! Kids master the new technologies with ease and communicate instantly via online social media sites, internet chat rooms, and mobile phone text messaging.

Yet, here on my doormat was a real, old-fashioned letter. Handwritten, no postcode. I scrutinized the writing. I can usually recognize a friend's handwriting before even opening the letter, but this hand was totally unknown to me. Intrigued, I ripped open the envelope and read the contents. It was dated April 22, 2001, and was from an address in North Wales.

Dear Julie

I have been trying to trace you & Jill, daughters of my youngest sister. I believe she was married to Ron School (actually Thomas Roy Wolsey Schoolar) of Lenton, Nottingham? My sister was called Audrey or Lilian, but I did not know her surname at the time. I have been given your address by your stepsister who lives in Calverton.

If this information means anything to you, would you like to give me a ring on the phone number above, also if you have information about Audrey or Lilian. I believe she married a man named Goodwin about 1972. It would be quicker if you phoned but I will enclose a stamped addressed envelope if needed, especially if you are not on the phone. This is not any bad news, on the contrary it will be good news for you and yours.

Hoping this short letter reaches you.

From your mother's eldest sister

–Joan

I was intrigued. I knew my mother had two sisters, but I had no recollection of ever meeting them. Why was Joan trying so desperately to trace us now? Why had she not been able to find my mother? When I told her that I had not had any contact with my mother for thirty years, what would she think of me?

In retrospect, if I had known the emotional roller-coaster ride that awaited me, the disillusionment with myself, with others and with the establishment, and how the strength of my relationships with family and friends would be put to the test, would I have torn the letter up and got on with my life?

But I could not have known. I picked up the telephone and dialed Joan's number.

CHAPTER 2
Memories

THE TELEPHONE CONVERSATION THAT ENSUED was understandably stilted. Here were two total strangers speaking to each other for the first time, and yet there was an immediate bond due to the family connection. I had experienced this same kind of instant affinity when Jill had first contacted me.

I confirmed to Joan that I was indeed Lilian Audrey Schoolar's eldest daughter, and hence her niece, that I had been in contact with my sister Jill since 1982, but that I had not seen or heard from my mother for thirty years, just prior to her marriage to Herbert Goodwin in 1972. She was living in Kirkby-in-Ashfield near Mansfield, Nottinghamshire, at that time.

Joan told me that Audrey had two sisters, herself and Dorothy, and a brother John. Their mother had died of tuberculosis in 1933, when my mother was just a babe in arms, and their father had placed all four of his children in the care of a privately run charitable institution in Beeston, Nottingham (originally called The Orphanage, but later called the Children's Homes, Beeston). At that time, Joan would have been eight, Dorothy seven; John five; and my mother less than two years old.

Joan spoke about the hard life that they had in the Children's Homes (plural, I later learned, because it was segregated into two parts, one for the boys and one for the girls). Even brothers and sisters were allowed no contact except at mealtimes, when they ate in the same room but were not allowed to speak. She kept mentioning my mother, how tiny and fragile she had been; she had photographs which she would show me.

Joan spoke about Dorothy's life as a teacher, how dedicated she had been to her chosen profession and how much she loved her work. Dorothy died of cancer in 1999. Joan had just cremated her husband Leslie when she had to rush down to London from Wales to be with Dorothy. Sadly, she was too late. Dorothy died the day Joan arrived in London.

Joan was left with the task of sorting out Dorothy's estate whilst still reeling from her own husband's death. Shortly after her arrival in London, Joan stumbled into the first solicitor's office she came across to ask for assistance with sorting out Dorothy's affairs. It should be quite a simple matter. Dorothy had lived at Carey Mansions in Westminster; a rather grand-sounding address, but in reality a council flat which she had rented for around thirty years. Dorothy had always lived frugally, but even Joan was shocked by the sparseness of her living accommodation on this, her final visit. Everything seemed in need of replacement or renewal. Dorothy had obviously spent nothing on the place for years.

Having lost her husband and sister in such quick succession, Joan's thoughts turned to tracing the only family she had left, her long-lost brother and sister. She wanted them to know of Dorothy's death and benefit from her inheritance. Dorothy had always been more inclined to save money than to spend it, so there would almost certainly be a considerable amount to share.

Quite a lot of this was news to me. I had not realized that my mother had a brother. My father had spoken of her sisters, but never of a brother. I also did not realize that her mother had died when she was so young and that she had therefore spent so much of her childhood in an institution. I had always known her as Audrey Freeman and did not realize that her real name was Mary Green. She had apparently been adopted in 1945 at thirteen years of age, and at that time, her name was changed from Gladys Mary Green to Lilian Audrey Freeman by the couple who adopted her, William Arthur and Lilian May Freeman.

I knew she lived with a couple for a while, whom I assumed were foster parents. My grandmother had told me that, as my mother got older, Mr. Freeman had started to "interfere" with her, and that is why she had left. The now common phrase "child abuse" had not been coined at this time. People only spoke of such things in hushed tones. I think my grandmother believed Audrey's claim, but there were no channels open to children then to report such things, and often if they did, they were not believed.

It had never occurred to me that the Freemans had legally adopted my mother. That being the case, William and Lilian Freeman were my grandparents, but I had never met them. I began to feel a sense of unease at the realization that I actually knew very little about my own mother.

In the days and weeks that followed this first conversation with Joan, I allowed myself to delve deep into the recesses of my mind to retrieve the few distant memories I had of my mother. I remembered the little house we lived in at Spring Close, Lenton. My father, who had six sisters and a brother, was brought up just around the corner on Commercial Street. In keeping with its name, there were terraced houses down one side of the street, factories and industrial units down much of the other side, and Simms Sons and Cooke, a wood yard, at the bottom of the street. It was a very close-knit community.

I never felt completely secure with my mother. This wasn't because she abused me in any way, but because she was rather childlike herself, and even as a toddler I sensed this. Perhaps I never truly bonded with her because apparently, she had a mental breakdown shortly after my birth and my grandparents, Bernard and Lucy, looked after me whilst she was in hospital. Once, when she was home from hospital on a visit, she had come to see me at my grandparents' house and had lifted me out of my cot. Evidently unaccustomed to handling a baby, to my grandmother's horror, Audrey clumsily dropped me onto the hard quarry tiled floor.

For the next few years, Audrey continued to suffer from severe mental illness. She was in and out of psychiatric hospitals, so I probably spent as much time with my grandparents and my dad's two younger sisters and brother who were still living at home, as I did with my actual parents.

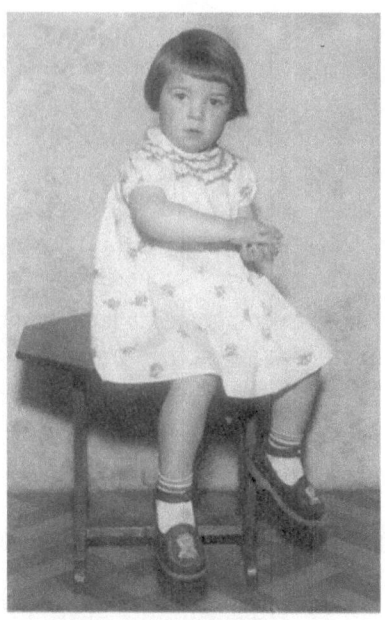

My most vivid memory is of a photographer coming to the house offering to take snaps of children. Few people had their own cameras in those days and so were often quite keen to avail themselves of this service. I remember my mother sitting me at a little table to pose for a photograph. I must have looked rather glum because she and the photographer went to great pains to amuse me and make me smile.

Their ultimate attempt was to keep throwing my teddy bear to each other across the room. I was not amused by their antics at all, so in the photograph I remain rather sullen. (My father must have given a copy of this photo to my grandmother because he wrote on it, "To Mam, from Roy and Audrey, Mother's Day 1957." This makes it easy to ascertain that I was two years and eight months of age in the photo, as I was born in July 1954.

My father used to get up for work in the morning, and I would come downstairs with him. He often made himself bacon and egg and would sit me on his knee whilst he ate his breakfast, feeding me pieces of bread dipped in the soft yolk of the egg. His chest and arms were very hairy, and I liked his smell. I felt very secure with him, but in those days, men didn't stay at home to care for their children. Whether my mother was still in bed at these times or undergoing treatment in a psychiatric hospital, I have no idea.

Family members have since told me that Audrey made several suicide attempts during times of depression when I was a toddler, although I was too young to be aware of this. She usually tried to gas herself, a common way of ending it all before we were all converted to North Sea gas. My great-grandmother, Mrs. Toplis, a very austere woman who lived a few doors from my grandparents on Commercial Street, had no sympathy with Audrey whatsoever. "She knows how far to go" was her verdict.

Eventually, the hospital suggested a leucotomy (lobotomy) might be the best treatment for my mother's acute anxiety and crippling depressions.

In his 1996 best-selling book on emotional intelligence, Daniel Goleman speaks in hindsight about "the advent in the 1940s of that rather desperate—and sadly misguided— 'cure' for mental illness: the prefrontal lobotomy, which (often sloppily) removed part of the prefrontal lobes or otherwise cut connections between the prefrontal cortex and the lower brain. In the days before any effective medications for mental illness, the lobotomy was hailed as the answer to grave emotional distress—sever the links between the prefrontal lobes and the rest of the brain and patients' distress was 'relieved.' Unfortunately, the cost was that most of the patients' emotional lives seemed to vanish, too. The key circuitry had been destroyed."

By the late 1940s or early 50s, the medical profession started to note the downside of this drastic medical procedure as shown by the quote below, and the prefrontal lobotomy began to wane in popularity.

"These patients are not only no longer distressed by their mental conflicts but also seem to have little capacity for any emotional experiences—pleasurable or otherwise. They are described by the nurses and the doctors, over and over, as dull, apathetic, listless, without drive or initiative, flat, lethargic, placid, and unconcerned, childlike, docile, needing pushing, passive, lacking in spontaneity, without aim or purpose, preoccupied and dependent" (Hoffmann 1949).

However, my parents were evidently so desperate for some improvement in my mother's condition that they decided to go ahead with it.

In some respects, the operation was a success, in that it did seem to curb my mother's severe depressions and suicide attempts. However, it changed her personality completely. Whereas prior to the operation she had been very concerned about her appearance, the appearance of the house, and what people thought of her, now she became unkempt, almost sluttish. She would also say the most inappropriate and hurtful things to people.

Sometime before or shortly after the operation, my sister Jill was born. She is two years younger than me. Due to Audrey's severe mental illness and the fact that she could barely cope with the child she already had, adoption was considered. My father no doubt felt that it was too much to expect his parents to raise another child, so he agreed to this.

He would return from work at midday and find Audrey still in bed or return at night to find no dinner ready. He came home one night to find there was a meal prepared, but it was all dry and burned up in the oven whilst Audrey was at a neighbour's house talking. He took the plate of unappetizing food to their house and asked if they considered that was a fit meal for a working man to come home to.

The roles of men and women were much more clearly defined in those days. The men went to work to provide for the family, and the women stayed at home to care for the children and keep house. My grandmother was an exceptional woman. She had brought up eight children, three of whom were still at home. She worked part-time as a cleaner at the nearby Nottingham University, and yet would consider she had failed in her duty as a wife if she didn't have her husband's dinner out on the table as he walked in the door from work. No wonder my father thought himself hard done to!

In truth, it couldn't have been easy for him. He and my mother married in 1951, both aged twenty. He was therefore still a very young man when his wife was suffering severe depression and attempting suicide. People who suffer mental illness rarely receive much sympathy or understanding, and in the 1940s, attitudes were even less enlightened. I think in the end my father just despaired of Audrey ever getting any better.

When I was five, things finally came to a head, like a malignant boil that must ultimately erupt, spewing out all the hurt, the distrust, the disappointment, the despair which have been festering below the surface for so long, poisoning the lifeblood of the relationship. I vaguely remember the resulting row. Lots of shouting, anger, accusations, hate. My mother was leaving, and I was crying hysterically, uncontrollably. My father turned to me and slapped me sharply across the face to bring me out of it. Now only sobbing, sharp intakes of breath as the tears run down my cheeks, and finally sleep.

The next morning, my father strapped my bed and mattress to a flat cart with two wheels, which belonged to my grandfather, hoisted me on top and trundled around the corner and down Commercial Street to my grandparents' house. It was already home-from-home to me, and he told me that I would be living with them permanently from then on.

Many years later, I learned from my father's youngest sister, Aunt Glenys, what had been the catalyst for this terrible argument. My mother had apparently promised me a party for my fifth birthday, although I have no recollection of this. On the day, she must have realized she was not up to the task or maybe even forgotten it altogether and she apparently took me out, so that when the local children she had invited started to arrive, there was nobody at home and no party! Word quickly got back to my grandparents, who informed my father. He was very angry, but I think this was more out of embarrassment at being shown up in front of the neighbours than because Audrey had reneged on her promise to me. If my father had been primarily concerned about my feelings, surely he wouldn't have staged that climactic row in front of me?

Soon after my mother left, my grandmother organized a big party for me and all the kids on the street were invited. I enjoyed it but still didn't understand what all the fuss had been about.

A year or so later, we had to leave 35 Commercial Street, the rented three-story terraced house where my grandparents had raised their eight children. The site was being cleared to make way for the construction of the Queen's Medical Centre, a huge teaching hospital. We were allocated a council house. It was only about a mile away geographically, but it felt as though we had moved to another world, as all our new neighbours were strangers to us.

Sometime after we moved, I was playing in the street with other children when a car pulled up. My mother was in the car with a man, a boyfriend I suppose. She called me over, but I was reluctant to go too close. I had it in my mind that they might pull me into the car and drive away with me. My grandmother had drummed it into me never to speak to strange men and never to get into a car with one.

In hindsight, I realize that Audrey had no intention of abducting me. They had probably simply been driving by and Audrey would have told her boyfriend to make a quick diversion on the off chance of seeing me, as like most kids in the early 1960s I spent much of my time playing in the street with other children from the neighbourhood. After a few minutes of coercing me, during which time the boyfriend looked decidedly uncomfortable at the spectacle of a child so wary of approaching her own mother, they drove away again, and I went back to my playmates and immersed myself in whatever game we were currently playing.

Looking back on this incident, it seems strange now that my mother never got out of the car. The possible reason for this became known to me much later when I learned that I have another half-sister, Denise, who is nine years and nine months younger than me. I think my mother may have been noticeably pregnant at this time, hence why she did not get out of the car, and that the boyfriend was most likely Denise's father— but more on this later.

My grandmother once told me that whilst Audrey was away so much in hospital, Roy started to go for dancing lessons. Apparently, Audrey loved dancing and always complained that my father wasn't good at it. He said he wanted to surprise her when she was finally well enough for them to go out on the town together.

That time never came, but through his dancing lessons my father met Eileen, who a few years later was to become my stepmother. They married when my father's divorce finally came through. I was seven or eight. I wasn't invited to the registry office wedding, but soon afterwards, I asked my father if I would be going to live with him again. He said that he and Eileen needed a few months to adjust to married life, but that after that I would be going to live with them. I often wondered why this never happened.

Sometime after the divorce, Audrey turned up to see me. I was sleeping over at a friend's house, so my grandparents allowed her to have my bed and wait to see me the following morning. Upon my return home, I was sent up to the bedroom to wake her up. Audrey asked me to get into bed with her and cuddled me. I'm sad to say that I felt distinctly uncomfortable, as though I was being intimate with a stranger, no doubt because I had seen my mother very infrequently since the day she walked out. Months and months would go by with no sign of her, and when she did turn up, it was always completely unexpected.

As we lay together, Audrey told me that Eileen had taunted her before the marriage breakup, saying that Roy was going to leave her and take me with him. This played on my mind for a long time afterwards. I thought my father was perfect and found it hard to accept that he had even known Eileen before the break-up of his marriage to my mother.

Later that day, before Audrey left, I told her that if she couldn't come to see me regularly, it would be better if she didn't come at all. I was eight years old. My grandmother was sitting in the room smoking a cigarette. The only time she did sit down before she got quite old was on the pretext of having a cigarette. She remained hopelessly addicted to them until she died at seventy-three years of age. She was already developing a smoker's cough, and she coughed now, but it was one of those little coughs born out of nervous embarrassment, when you think you should say something, but you don't know what. Audrey looked puzzled for a moment, and then said that she wondered who would put it into my head to say such a thing. In truth, no one had, but it must have been hard for her to accept that a child could be so forthright in expressing what they did and didn't want. She left, and I didn't see her again until I was seventeen years old.

I never forgot what Audrey had said about Eileen making the taunt that my father was going to leave her and take me with him. Sometime later—I really can't remember if it was months or years—I was staying with my dad and Eileen for some reason. There must have been a special reason because I didn't normally stay with them. My father would visit me at weekends at his parents' house.

My father went to work every day, which meant I spent a lot of time alone with Eileen. I always felt she barely tolerated me. Prior to her marriage to my father, we had spent quite a lot of time together.

They would go on day trips and take me and Eileen's youngest brother, Alan, who was only a few years older than me. After their marriage, however, and particularly when Eileen had children of her own (my two half-sisters and a half-brother), I seemed to be less and less a part of their lives.

On one of those endlessly long days which we spent together, I simply had to broach the subject. I told Eileen that Audrey had accused her of saying that Roy was going to leave her and take me with him.

"That's utter rubbish," came the terse reply, "because I never had any intention of having you."

I wondered whether my father had known that before he married my stepmother and felt a bit betrayed.

CHAPTER 3
A visit to meet Aunt Joan

I SPOKE WITH JOAN ON the telephone most weeks after our initial conversation, and it wasn't long before Jill and I made arrangements to pay her a visit. Jill was as intrigued as I was to meet our long-lost aunt. We decided to visit in May for a few days.

It was nice to spend some time exclusively with Jill as we drove the two hundred miles from Nottingham to North Wales to visit Joan. I had known I had a sister since my grandmother told me about her when I was seven years of age, but it had been wonderful to actually meet her and get to know her personally after receiving a letter from her in 1982. Naturally, during the first few years after our reunion, we spent a lot of time getting to know each other. The relationship was very special to me.

Jill had been adopted by a couple called Jack and Margaret. Jack was a coal miner, a thriving industry in Nottingham in the 1950s. They lived at the end one of a row of four miners' cottages in Gedling village, which they later bought. They had already adopted another girl, Rosemary. Margaret rang up the Social Services and expressed an interest in adopting another child. "We have a girl and a boy at the moment" was the reply. "You'd better come along and take your pick." They "picked" Jill, a baby just a few months old. If this account of events is correct, one has to marvel at how much the adoption system has tightened up! Yet it still goes horribly wrong at times.

Jill told me that she had enjoyed an idyllic childhood. A bit of a tomboy, she had spent most of her time climbing trees and getting into various scrapes. She has memories of family squabbles between Jack and Margaret whilst she and Rosemary were growing up, usually on a Sunday over Jack staying too long at the pub, but Jill certainly seems to have felt secure in her adoptive parents' love.

Always a bright child, as she entered her teens, they suggested that Jill should be thinking about working in an office rather than a factory. Jill retorted, "Work in an office? I want to go to university!" This was quite something in the early 1970s, for the daughter of a working-class couple to have her sights set on a university education. Once they saw how committed to the idea Jill was, Jack and Margaret gave her their full support. Jill took her A levels and gained entry to Leeds University to study English.

Jill met her future husband Glyn whilst working as a "red coat" at Butlin's holiday camp to earn some money during the long summer break from university. He wasn't an academic but had tremendous social skills, which would ensure he got on in life. By an amazing coincidence, Glyn's family lived in Leeds, so when Jill returned to university, they continued seeing each other and later married. After Jill graduated from university, they settled in Nottingham. Jill went into teaching, specializing in English and drama.

I was tremendously proud of Jill and all she had accomplished. I was sad that our father was no longer alive to hear how well she had done. I knew that he would be proud of her too. I was quite bright for the times and left school at sixteen with six GCE O levels and a few CSEs and got a job in an office. However, in my final two years at school, I can remember my stepmother Eileen saying to my grandmother that she hoped I wasn't planning to go on to college because it was a real struggle for Roy to keep paying toward my keep, although I believe he paid a very modest amount. However, by now they had three children of their own to provide for. The thought of furthering my education had never occurred to me, but in hindsight, it would have been nice to at least be encouraged to think about it.

Naturally, shortly after I met Jill, the subject came up of whether to try to contact our mother. I hadn't seen Audrey since 1971 when I was seventeen years of age. At forty, Audrey had finally settled down with a fifty-seven-year-old widower, Herbert Goodwin. She had told him about her past life and that she had a daughter who would now be in her teens. I assume he encouraged her to seek me out. They visited my father at the Eastcroft depot on London Road where he worked for the Nottingham Corporation. This was something of an embarrassment to my father, who had climbed the ladder from lowly mechanic to a managerial position. Audrey said that she wanted to see me. Roy told her he would speak with me and see if he could arrange something.

My father passed Audrey's address on to me. She was living about fifteen miles away in Kirkby-in-Ashfield. I decided I would pay her a visit, and Steve took me on the little two stroke motorbike he had renovated. Although he was twenty and I was only seventeen, we were already engaged and planned to marry in a few months' time.

We found the council flats where Audrey and Herbert were living and knocked. Audrey came to the door. She was still very petite, as I remembered her, but looking older than her forty years and rather dowdy, mainly because she had lost all her teeth and had not replaced them with dentures. She expressed surprise and pleasure at seeing me and invited us in. Herbert, who was fifty-seven, seemed a very old man to my young eyes. "Well, Audrey, you'd better put the kettle on," he suggested good-naturedly.

As the little tea-making ritual progressed, I glanced around the flat. They possessed only the most basic furniture, and it wasn't particularly tidy or well kept, yet Audrey and Herbert seemed happy and relaxed in each other's company. Attempts were made at polite conversation, but what was there to say? When Audrey started to question my forthcoming marriage at such a young age, I thought she had a cheek. What right had she got to be advising me on how to live my life? She hadn't been around for most of it!

We probably stayed for no more than an hour. Toward the end of the visit, Herbert suggested that it would be nice if Audrey could be at my wedding. I cringed inwardly at the thought of the embarrassment this would cause, not only to me, but to my dad, his second wife, and the rest of his family. None of them had ever had a good word to say about Audrey, particularly after the breakup of their marriage. Mainly, though, I was thinking of myself. I wouldn't be proud to introduce this dowdy little woman to Steve's family and our friends as my mother. I took a deep breath, "Look, I'm pleased to have seen you and glad that you're happy and settled, but I don't really see any point in keeping in touch after all these years."

Audrey sat speechless, as she had done when I rejected her for the first time nine years previously. Herbert waited for a moment or two then remarked quietly, "You know, Julie, it's a terrible thing to turn your back on your mother."

As it happens, I had to eat humble pie shortly afterwards. Our wedding date was set for October 2, and Steve and I went to the registrar's office to finalize our plans a few weeks after our visit to see my mother. As I was under eighteen years of age, the lady registrar said that I would need to get a form signed by both my parents to indicate their agreement to my marriage. I told her that I hardly knew my mother but had been raised by my grandparents after she and my father divorced. However, the registrar explained that if I had seen my mother in the last eight years and knew of her whereabouts, I must get her signature on that form or there could be no wedding until I was eighteen. Only a few weeks prior to this, I could honestly say that I hadn't seen Audrey for over eight years and had no idea of her whereabouts! How inconvenient that she had decided to show up again at this crucial time. Rather than change our plans at this late stage, I decided I would simply have to pay my mother another visit and ask if she would give her consent. My father agreed to accompany me, and we drove there in his car. He had contacted Audrey and explained the reason for our visit beforehand.

After some polite conversation, Roy asked whether she had decided to give her consent or not. Audrey hesitated for a moment - I think she was actually enjoying being the one in control for a change - then she said that she would sign the consent form because she loved me and wanted me to be happy. I was totally unmoved by this statement. My only thought was to get out of that flat before she changed her mind.

As Dad drove back home, I sat beside him in the car, clutching the signed consent form. He suggested that my stepmother Eileen would probably have more interest in the wedding if my half-sister Ellen could be a bridesmaid. I said that would be okay.

I sent a couple of wedding photographs to Audrey, of course. She let me know that she and Herbert married six months later in March 1972, and she got herself some dentures in time for the occasion. After that, I never heard from her again.

So, when the subject came up of Jill and me tracing our mother, I wasn't particularly encouraging. I thought that Jill could only be disappointed, even ashamed of Audrey, as I had been. There was another consideration. Jill's adoptive father had died, but Margaret, her adoptive mother, was still alive. She had accepted Jill searching and finding her sister, but how would she react if she knew Jill was searching for her birth mother? After all, you can have a number of sisters, but you generally only have one mother. We decided not to go ahead with it.

Jill and I had been particularly close when her husband Glyn died of a brain hemorrhage in 1993. Steve and I were living in Scotland at the time when we heard the tragic news. Glyn was only forty years of age, and they had a five-year-old adopted son, Iain. Glyn had a secure job as a sales manager, Jill had cut down to teaching part-time after they adopted Iain, and they were now considering adopting another child. Life was good, then suddenly...

Shortly after Glyn's death, Steve and I decided to return to Nottingham. We had never managed to make ends meet financially in the four years we lived in Scotland, and although we loved the area, it was obviously necessary to be able to pay your way. Glyn's death had also brought home to us the importance of family, and we decided that we wanted to be nearer Steve's elderly parents and on hand to give Jill and Iain our support.

Nine years had now passed since Glyn's death, and Jill had shown tremendous strength of character in getting on with her life. She had continued to teach and in addition to that had totally immersed herself in bringing Iain up single-handedly. He must have been a member of every after-school club going, including cubs and later scouts. They were always busy doing something or going on holiday abroad somewhere. I remember one evening, around two years after Glyn had died, Jill and Iain had been over to our house for the evening. Jill was washing up after dinner and humming to herself. After they left, Steve remarked that this was the first time he had heard Jill humming, whistling, or singing since Glyn's death. We both felt that, hopefully, she was coming to the end of the grieving process, and her life could move on.

Over the years, I feel Jill and I began to drift apart. Iain was now a teenager, boarding midweek at a private school and busy with his friends at the weekends. Jill had started to rekindle her social life, going out with a circle of mainly divorced or single girlfriends. Steve and I had little money for holidays or other social activities and were struggling to pay a mortgage on a modest house we had bought since our return to Nottingham. We had settled into a routine of cozy domesticity, and our lives were very different to Jill's. The arrival of our long-lost Aunt Joan on the scene therefore gave Jill and I a common focus of interest.

Joan lives in Tallybont, Gwynedd, a little village about four miles from Barmouth on the west coast of North Wales. Barmouth is a typical seaside town with amusements, a fun fair, donkey rides on the beach, etc. Tallybont is just a short distance away with some beautiful, relatively secluded beaches of its own. Joan and her husband Leslie had bought a bungalow thirty years previously and moved to live there permanently when Leslie retired. Several of Joan's neighbours are also retired people from England, and she seems to fit in very well.

Jill and I made the most of our journey, stopping off at a pub for some lunch on the way. The sun was shining, so we were able to sit outside and enjoy the scenery on the road between Shrewsbury and Welshpool. Once we got to Barmouth, we telephoned Joan to tell her that we would shortly be arriving. As we turned into her road, we saw our Aunt Joan for the first time, hurrying along the pavement excitedly to meet us. We wound the window down to take her instructions as to which bungalow to park outside.

What a character Joan turned out to be! Born in 1925, she is very feisty for her years. I suppose she could well be described as a loveable eccentric. She keeps herself up to date with world events by avidly reading the newspapers every day, and she has quite strong views and opinions on most issues. These are often opposite to what you would expect from a woman of her generation. For example, she is an atheist and an anti-royalist. She also believes passionately in euthanasia, that people should be able to terminate their own lives if they so wish.

The few days we spent with her were very enjoyable. We chauffeured her around, as she showed us the best local beaches, the castle nearby at Harlech, and came with us on a trip to Portmeirion where the cult series *The Prisoner* had been filmed in the 1960s.

We had a meal out one evening at a Bistro in Harlech. Whilst visiting the castle, we had taken a look at the place, seen what time it opened, and studied the menus, which were posted up in the windows. I had already decided to have the Welsh lamb and stuck to my choice despite Jill commenting on the way to the restaurant how delightful the baby lambs were gamboling around in the fields. Joan insisted on paying for everything, as she was so delighted to have tracked her two nieces down at long last.

During the course of the visit, we spent a lot of time talking to Joan about their life as children in the orphanage and mulling over old photographs, letters, and documents. I found it particularly fascinating to learn about our other aunt, Dorothy, who had died in 1999. She had never married or had children but had been completely devoted to her career as a nursery and then primary schoolteacher. For the last twenty-four years before her retirement in 1985, she taught at Yerbury Primary School, Upper Holloway, N19. Joan had photos, letters, and other personal effects which she had brought home after clearing Dorothy's flat out.

Dorothy had lived a very frugal life, never spending very much money on herself. Even so, it came as an utter shock to Joan to find that when all Dorothy's affairs were sorted, her estate amounted to £360,000 after deduction of inheritance tax. Joan said that her reason for tracing her brother John and later attempting to trace our mother was because she wanted them both to share in Dorothy's inheritance.

Her brother John had been found quite easily. Joan had not seen him since he went into the navy around 1943. Joan hadn't seen her youngest sister, our mother, since the mid to late 1950s. Both Joan and Dorothy had been at Audrey's wedding to our father in 1951, and Joan had a photograph. She also remembered coming to my grandparents' house at 35 Commercial Street after the wedding and visiting Audrey in her own house around the corner on Spring Close when I was just a babe in arms. However, after she left my father in the late 1950s, my mother drifted around a lot and lost contact with both her sisters.

Joan had arranged for us to stay in a nearby guesthouse, as she only had one spare bedroom with a three-quarter sized bed in it. So, after a night of studying old photographs and recalling distant memories, Jill and I made our way back to our lodgings. I remarked how much I would have loved to meet Dorothy. I felt an affiliation with her, a certainty that she and I would have got on really well.

My parents' wedding in 1951. From left to right: Joan, Sam (best man), Roy and Audrey, my grandparents Lucy and Bernard, and Dorothy.

I was taken aback when Jill said that she had been quite hurt that evening by Aunt Joan and me discussing "happy childhood memories" which she had no part in, having been adopted. I told her that any childhood memories I had were far from happy, and that, from what she had told me about her own childhood, being adopted had been the very best thing which could have happened to her.

I had always envied the upbringing Jill had experienced. In ways I wished I had also been adopted by a couple who really wanted me.

I had felt betrayed and rejected when my newly married father and stepmother did not invite me to go to live with them, and although I have no doubt that my grandparents genuinely cared about me, I always felt like a spare piece of furniture in their house, too good to throw out but nonetheless surplus to requirements, a bit in the way. It had not occurred to me that Jill might at times struggle with the fact that she had been given away for adoption whilst the family had found a way to keep me.

Before we left to return to Nottingham, at Joan's request, we made a telephone call to her solicitor.

Her brother John, after he was traced, had informed Joan that their youngest sister Mary (Audrey) had been adopted and was "no longer of the family." He felt it was therefore pointless trying to find her because she wasn't eligible to inherit any of Dorothy's estate under the intestacy laws. This had taken Joan aback because she did not realize their youngest sister had been legally adopted. Like me, Joan regarded the Freemans as foster parents. However, further searches revealed that Audrey had indeed been legally adopted at thirteen years of age, and even though it had not worked out and she ran away from her adoptive parents when she was fifteen, this brief adoption annulled her right to a share in Dorothy's estate. The inheritance had therefore been divided equally between Joan and John. However, Joan was very upset by John's harsh attitude toward their youngest sister, dismissing her as "no longer of the family" and not wishing to trace her. Joan was back in contact with her brother John after fifty-six years, but sadly, before they even met face-to-face, this drove a wedge between them.

Shortly after they each received their half of Dorothy's estate, Joan wrote the following letter to her brother dated April 3, 2000:

> *To John and his Family,*
>
> *By now you will have no doubt received poor Dot's money. Again I repeat if it had not been for me you would not have received it as she had left an old Will—leaving it to me and the man she had lived with for years—he had died before her so it could have all come to me. It was then decided that as she had torn up the Will she had died intestate…*
>
> *When I phoned you, you were so full of your own miserable childhood you never wanted to know about us! We all had a hard time, especially poor little Audrey Mary Gladys. Which name she kept I do not know. Hers was one of the saddest, as she was only a baby when our mother died. I have begun to try to find out if she is still alive. I have found so far that she had married twice and had two girls; yes she was adopted but she was unhappy with them and came back to us. She married early but was unstable and left her child with her husband— she took herself off and Dot told me she drifted. Anyway she had another marriage and another child who I'm trying to trace…*
>
> *I would love to give her a helping hand, or her children, and that's why I suggested you split the money three ways but*

you were adamant that you would not go along with this. I hope you can still live with yourself, or it may be the influence of your family, who knows...But I shall continue to try and trace Audrey, or her children and I may use publicity to do this. I will not spend the money as I am too old to change my lifestyle...

True to her word, Joan had indeed found us, a year after she wrote this letter. Now she wanted her solicitor to contact John again and ask him if he would be prepared to voluntarily and without coercion return a third of the money he had received for the benefit of his sister Mary, if she could be traced, or her daughters. Joan would do the same, as she felt this is what Dorothy would have wanted.

Joan's solicitor agreed to draft a letter to John Green, and Jill and I returned to Nottingham. I knew I had to set about trying to trace my mother in earnest. This is something which I had been meaning to do for about the last ten years. I felt that now, in my forties and having raised my daughter, I finally had the emotional maturity needed to develop a relationship with my own mother.

Since Joan contacted me, I had learnt so much about Audrey's tragic life, which I never knew before. I could now understand that, never having experienced a mother's love, she was simply incapable of being a mother herself. But how was I going to find her?

CHAPTER 4
Aunt Dorothy

UPON MY RETURN TO NOTTINGHAM, despite being thrown back into the busy work routine, I was determined to get the ball rolling in the search for my mother. I'd put it off for far too long already.

I was a fairly new Internet user, but it was about to prove an invaluable asset. Searching under "missing persons," I was put in touch with a company who specialized in finding people. I commissioned a search of the 2001 electoral register for Lilian A. Goodwin.

Some weeks later, they reported back to me. In the whole of the UK, there were no matches for Lilian A. Goodwin, but twenty-eight for Lilian Goodwin. Only two of these were in the Nottingham area, but I assumed she could be anywhere in the UK, particularly if her second husband, Herbert, had died. He had seemed so old to me when I met him as a seventeen-year-old, surely he couldn't still be alive? Audrey was forty when she remarried in 1972. That meant she would be seventy now. Herbert was seventeen years her senior, so he would be eighty-seven. I suppose it was possible he might still be alive. I put a brief letter together and posted it to the twenty-eight addresses for Lilian Goodwin with a mixture of hope, excitement, and trepidation. Would my search be successful?

In the meantime, Joan had let me bring home some documents, photographs, and letters, which she had acquired whilst clearing out Dorothy's flat, and I spent a long time perusing these whilst I waited for replies to my letter. How I wished I had known Aunt Dorothy!

Photographs showed that, in her younger days, she had been very slim and pretty, although in later life she put on quite a lot of weight. After she had been diagnosed with cancer, from which she died in 1999, she had attempted to compile a family history.

The narrative that follows is based on information gleaned from Dorothy's memoirs:-

According to their marriage certificate, Walter Edwin Green and Olive Minnie Poole married on July 12, 1924, at Paddington Register

Office. Walter was twenty-nine and Olive twenty-eight. They were both in residence at 4 Hyde Park Gardens. Walter's occupation is shown as "Butler".

Their respective fathers, John James Green, a sanitary engineer and Dansie Carter Pool, a draper, are both shown as deceased. Olive had six sisters but no brothers. What brought them to Nottinghamshire? Their second child, Dorothy Olive Green, born in 1926, takes up the story...

"When my mother married my father, her family turned her out from her home in Finsbury Park, London, because they did not want her to marry my father. They went to live in a council house in Warsop, near Mansfield, and my father became a miner. Before they left London my eldest sister, Joan, was born in Saint Charlottes Hospital, Hammersmith. Only one of my mother's sisters came to see her in Warsop to give her money and her son's clothes for my brother, John. I saw my aunt when she came to Warsop, but she only came the one time, and my mother never saw her again.

"My father had very little money, and he turned to drink and deprived my mother of many things. I remember trying to stop my father from beating my mother. They had no telephone or refrigerator and very little furniture, so life was very bleak for my mother. I always remember her cooking, cleaning, and washing. My father never mentioned anything about his family, and we never saw anyone related to him, and so my mother lived a very lonely life in Warsop. She had my eldest sister Joan in 1925, I was born in 1926, and my brother John in 1928. My sister and I went to school in Warsop. At the age of five, I became very ill at school with pains in my stomach. My mother took me home in an old pram and called the doctor. He told my mother to feed me on baked custard and left. When my father came home, he could see I was very ill and called an ambulance. They took me to a Nottingham hospital, and the surgeon had to operate straight away because I had peritonitis. The surgeon said I was very lucky to survive.

"My father lost his job, and my mother had her last baby, Mary in 1931. The nurse came to the house to deliver the baby girl, but my mother became very ill after this and she was very thin and emaciated, so they took her to hospital and the baby went with her. The hospital asked my father to bring his children to the hospital because my mother did not have long to live."

(*This "hospital" was in fact the infirmary at the Southwell Workhouse, now a museum, which had a special ward for tuberculosis patients.*)

"My mother asked me to kiss her, but I shook my head, so she gave me a biscuit. My baby sister was near the ward and an old lady put bread in her own mouth to soften it and gave it to my sister. I heard my mother say, 'What will happen to my children?' Because she looked so thin and ill I really did not recognize her. That was the last time I saw her except to go to the funeral, which was paid for by Nottingham City Council."

"My father was quite lost with four children, and he heard of an orphanage in Beeston near Nottingham. He went to see the lady who ran it, and she told him she would take us in if he contributed to our keep. My younger sister Mary stayed in hospital until she was old enough to join us"

"I remember how frightened I was when my father left us, and we were put in a playroom with other children. My brother John was separated from us, and he was put in the boy's half of the Homes. Boys and girls had meals together but never saw each other apart from this. We suffered very harsh treatment and our meals were very meagre."

"We had to get up at six o'clock and make our own beds, and if we were old enough, we had to clean the dormitory before breakfast. We had to stand in line waiting for breakfast until the bell rang and were not allowed to talk until breakfast was over. We were given a number for our coat pegs and lockers and our clothes. We were called by our number not our name."

A young Dorothy

"We never had fresh fruit and vegetables and one egg a year on Easter Sunday. We never had enough to eat, and when I was eleven, I was taken to the doctor because I was so thin the matron thought I had consumption, but it turned out to be lack of calcium. "When we were old enough, we did all the cleaning in the home and washing. We went to the local schools, and because we had to wear uniform, the children often called us names and would not play with us. I was very bright at school and my report was quite good, but the matron said, 'You will never get on because you come from the slums.'

DOROTHY OLIVE GREEN
1926–1999

I visited the Nottingham Archives and looked up the school admissions records. Dorothy was admitted to Church Street Primary School in Beeston in 1933 and in the comments column it says, "Very Backward." She was possibly traumatized by her mother's death, but apparently later did well at school, as she mentions. Dorothy left the Children's Home on Imperial Road, Beeston, in 1940 and went into training to become a nurse at the Firs Hospital in Nottingham. She had her accommodation and meals there but did not enjoy nursing and decided that she would like to become a primary/nursery teacher. She attended Didsbury College in Manchester for two years before taking up various teaching posts in Nottingham and later in London. She loved teaching and stayed in the profession until her retirement in 1985.

The photograph overleaf was taken at Thomas Wall Nursery School in Sutton, Surrey, in 1955. Dorothy is the teacher in the centre of the bottom row with a little girl sitting on her lap. I sent this to the *Sutton Post*, a local free newspaper, and they published the photograph on October 17, 2001, with the following dialogue: "A woman from Nottingham is appealing to readers for information about her aunt who died in 1999 and who she never knew. Julie Leek is hoping that people in Sutton will remember Dorothy Olive Green who worked at Thomas Wall Nursery School in the borough between 1952 and 1956. Julie Leek says, "I would love to hear from some of those children, their parents or any of Dorothy's former colleagues.'"

As a result, I received a letter from the teacher to her right, Mrs. Gwen Foy nee Chaston, who remembers Dorothy and has a copy of the identical photograph herself.

Before her retirement in 1985, Dorothy taught at Yerbury Infants School, Foxham Road, Upper Holloway, London for twenty-four years. She was for many years a much-valued member of staff, as evidenced by the following testimonial.

"Miss Green never discriminates, selects, rejects, or complains. All children are lovingly and caringly received, and she can boast of many successes, even triumphs, with those who have been very difficult to deal with...Miss Green has become an institution here, respected and affectionately regarded, and many, many children have started off on their educational progress under her aegis."

At a friend's suggestion, I once again utilized the internet to good effect. Having registered for membership of a website called Friends Reunited, I emailed all those listed who were at Yerbury during the years when Dorothy was teaching reception classes. My email was worded as follows:-

"I am wondering if you remember Miss Green, who taught reception classes at Yerbury Primary between 1961–1985 after which she retired.

Thomas Wall Nursery School, Sutton Surrey, 1955
Dorothy on the front row with a young girl on her knee

"She is my Aunt Dorothy, who died in 1999. Sadly, I never knew her. She was brought up in an orphanage in Nottingham with her two sisters and one brother after the tragic death of their mother in 1933. After they left the orphanage, she lost touch with her youngest sister, who was my mother. As I know so very little about her, anything which her former pupils may remember would be of interest to me."

To my great delight, I received a number of replies. Ananda Edwards, a former pupil, writes:

"Yes, I was taught by Miss Green, and she was one of the few teachers I actually liked! She was a really sweet lady who always had time for all the children. I was a bit of a tearaway at school and she would calm me down with a rich tea biscuit and orange squash. When there was the fire at Yerbury she was instrumental in getting all the children to safety at the Whittington Park Community Centre and making sure we were all right. We were doing PE at the time and it was pretty scary!"

This serious fire at the school took place in 1978. It caused huge disruption at the time and necessitated a great deal of reorganization afterwards. Memories of the fire are so vivid in people's minds, it is mentioned not only in Ananda's email, but also in both testimonials from former head teachers and also in a letter from Eve Smith, a former colleague of Dorothy's at Yerbury. I was put in touch with Eve Smith by Peter Hession, another former pupil who responded to my email.

Eve Smith's letter says, in part:

"Dorothy was a very private person and never spoke of her life outside school. She loved her job and there are so many people who will remember Miss Green with great affection. She created a warm and happy environment for the children in her care.

"I can't recall her ever being absent and even during a transport strike she walked all the way to and from school. (I think she was living in Westminster!!) She was always punctual and was frequently the last to leave at the end of the day.

"She was for many years the RE co-ordinator for the school, and it was obvious that she took strength from her faith. She occasionally took whole school assemblies and loved telling Bible stories in particular and she was able to keep the children enthralled. She loved the whole school singing sessions and sometimes played the piano. She knew all the hymns by heart and delighted in singing them with great gusto."

Never having met Aunt Dorothy, it meant a lot to me to hear from people who had actually known her, worked with her, or been taught by her. I felt incredibly proud of Dorothy and her ability, despite her own harsh experiences in the orphanage, to give the children she taught the loving encouragement she never received.

However, I feel that Dorothy was deeply affected by her upbringing, and this was possibly reflected in the way she never married or had children of her own, despite having a great love for children and living at a time when most women did marry and have a family. It seems she had men friends (Gwen Foy mentions a boyfriend in her letter) but could never make a long-term commitment to them.

In later years, a man-friend, Douglas Worsley, moved in with Dorothy at Carey Mansions, Westminster. They never married and, in many ways seem to have lived very separate lives. However, there was obviously a bond between them.

In 1985 Dorothy left Yerbury primary school, retiring slightly early. According to Joan, a new headteacher had come to the school with fresh ideas and considered Dorothy's methods old fashioned. Doughlas confided to Joan that leaving Yerbury had been totally devastating for Dorothy. Douglas died 5 years later in 1990.

*Dorothy with pupils at Yerbury Primary School
Foxham Road, Upper Holloway, London*

During the final years of her life, Dorothy lived very simply. She had always been careful with her finances, but during these latter years, it seems she became even more frugal, hence the amount of money she left when she died, despite never acquiring any property. Among Dorothy's papers, I found the following quote, which she had cut out of a magazine:-

"This is the greatest gift—to choose a life one can admire oneself for living"

I certainly admire Dorothy and hope that before her death she looked back on her life and the choices she had made with a sense of satisfaction and pride in what she had accomplished and the difference she had made to so many young lives.

CHAPTER 5
Sad News

STEPHEN AND I DECIDED TO take a run over to Kirkby-in-Ashfield to try to find the flats where Audrey and Herbert were living when we last paid them a visit. I couldn't remember the exact address. However, I had a copy of their 1972 marriage certificate which a search company had found whilst trying to trace Audrey on Joan's behalf and the address given for both of them when they married was 16 Darley Avenue. We found these Council flats, in blocks of four, two up, two down. No-one was in at No.16, so we knocked at the neighbours' doors and asked if any of them had any recollection of Mr & Mrs Goodwin, but no-one could tell us anything.

What a depressing place Kirkby-in-Ashfield is. An old mining town, it has never recovered from the closure of the coal pits and the decline of the industry which was its lifeblood.

I also started to make some enquiries relating to the Beeston Children's Homes where I now knew my mother, her brother and sisters had grown up. Dorothy's account of life at the Homes was fascinating, but I felt I needed a more rounded out view. I began contacting various agencies which I felt sure would be able to give me lots of historical information and background.

I rang the local Council, Broxtowe. They told me that the only information they had relating to the Childrens' Homes was an application for a change of use in the early 1960's. They suggested I contact Beeston Civic Society.

Mrs Joyce Cook was the secretary of Beeston Civic Society . She seemed fascinated by the story of my mother, aunts and uncle, and could vaguely remember the old orphanage. After a few weeks passed and I heard nothing, I decided to telephone Joyce Cook again. Sadly, her initial interest and enthusiasm seemed to have waned. She could, however, give me the telephone number of Margaret Cooper, a well-known local historian and member of the

Beeston Historical Society. She had published a book about the old Beeston village and doubtless knew everything there was to know about the Children's Homes.

When I first spoke to Margaret Cooper on the telephone, she misunderstood what I was talking about and started to tell me about the Silverwood Nursing Home for the elderly, which had been erected on the site of the old orphanage in the early 1990s. I interrupted her to explain that it was the original orphanage I was enquiring about, and she was able to tell me the following;-

The Children's Homes were founded in the 1880s by Miss Kate Bayley, the daughter of Sir H. D. Readett Bayley, and were run in conjunction with a day nursery on Heathcoat Street at Nottingham where working women were able to leave their children whilst they toiled in the nearby lace market factories. Both boys and girls boarded at the Homes, which were beautifully appointed with extensive grounds.

Ms. Cooper assured me that there was no stigma attached to being a resident at the Homes and the children were allowed to bring schoolmates home with them for tea and to play in the lovely gardens. I interjected that my mother, uncle, and two aunts had spent most of their childhood in the Homes. Not wanting to shatter the idyll Margaret Cooper was painting, which strongly contrasted with Dorothy's written memoirs and Joan's verbal recollections, I decided to mention that, upon leaving, my aunt Dorothy had become a teacher and my uncle John went into the legal profession and later the navy, and now had two children, one a barrister and another a doctor.

"Oh, jolly good, very well done," Margaret Cooper replied.

A few weeks had now passed since I sent out the twenty-eight letters to Lilian Freemans on the 2001 electoral roll. I had received seven replies, but none of them were from my mother. My search now had to take a new direction. I had to consider the possibility that my mother may be dead. I contacted the search company again and this time commissioned a search of the death register between 1984–99. However, my mother would only be seventy, no age at all these days, so I really didn't expect to hear bad news. A week or so later, I received their findings. There was only one match for this time period.

NAME: LILIAN AUDREY GOODWIN
DATE OF BIRTH: 9 AUGUST 1931
MONTH/YEAR OF DEATH: JUNE 1985
DISTRICT REGISTERED: NOTTINGHAM

I read the information again and again. The name was exactly correct, the district was Nottingham, but this could have been a coincidence. However, when I saw that the date of birth was correct, I knew it could only be my mother. Yet this death had occurred seventeen years ago, when she was only fifty-three years of age.

I went over and over in my mind what I was doing in 1985. We had returned to England from Eire in 1983 and were living back in Nottingham. My father had died five years previously at forty-nine years of age from throat cancer. I had been in touch with my sister Jill for three years. My daughter Emma was a thirteen-year-old teenager. I could now add to this list the fact that, unbeknown to me, my mother died that year.

I contacted the search company and asked them to order a copy of the death certificate. Had she, too, been a victim of cancer? That seemed the most likely explanation.

After a fortnight, the death certificate still had not arrived and I was getting agitated. A part of me still could not accept that my mother was really dead. The death certificate would give further proof one way or the other. I decided to travel into Nottingham during my lunch break from work and pay for a copy of the death certificate directly from the registrar's office on Shakespeare Street. A short wait and I would be able to take it away with me.

I arrived at the registrar's office, completed the paperwork with the necessary details, and waited. I was handed the certificate in a brown paper envelope and thanked the clerk. I decided to take a look before I left the office. The details were as follows:-

"Drowning having taken her own life whilst depressed" ...I read the words over and over several times. Knowing her nature, past depressions, and suicide attempts, of course I had always known this was a possibility. Now, faced with the reality that my mother had taken her own life, for the moment I felt only numbness. I approached the enquiry desk again. Of course, they knew the manner of her death. They had looked out the details and typed a copy of the certificate.

"Excuse me. This certificate says that my mother drowned. Is there any way I could find out more about her death?"

The gentlemen behind the desk seemed intent on not meeting my gaze but instead scrutinized the death certificate. "Well, it says there was an inquest and a coroner's report. I can give you the telephone number of the coroner's office if you would like to give them a ring."

Date and place of death:	Tenth June 1985
	Dead on arrival at University Hospital, Nottingham
Name and surname:	Lilian Audrey GOODWIN
Date and place of birth:	9 August 1931, Blidworth, Notts
Occupation/ usual address:	Widow of Herbert Goodwin, a machine turner, 6 Half Moon Drive, Kirkby-in-Ashfield
Name of Informant:	Certificate received from John Langham, Coroner for Nottinghamshire. Inquest held 19 June 1985
Cause of death:	Drowning having taken her own life whilst depressed

I walked out into the summer sunshine and headed in the direction of Parliament Street and toward my bus stop, but I knew I couldn't return to work that day. I sat down on a bench near the Theatre Royal and used my mobile phone to make a brief call to work telling them not to expect me back that afternoon. I didn't give any details. I didn't really care about justifying my absence at that moment. I sat on the bench, all the hustle and bustle of the city continuing unabated around me, yet I felt my life had come to a juddering halt whilst I was transported back to finally confront issues which I had shelved years before. An overwhelming feeling of sadness engulfed me. Tears welled up and ran down my cheeks. Seventeen years too late. I had begun to seriously consider trying to trace my mother about ten years ago, yet even then I was already too late.

Upon arriving home, I contacted the coroner's office and briefly explained who I was and that I had only just discovered that my mother had committed suicide in 1985. Would I be able to see the coroner's report into her death? I was told to put my request into writing and they would contact me. I wrote, in part:

> Dear Sirs —LILIAN AUDREY GOODWIN
>
> *I am the above person's daughter and I last saw my mother in 1971, just prior to her second marriage to Herbert Goodwin. At this time, we mutually agreed not to keep in touch. However, recently her eldest sister got in contact with me, and we have been trying to trace Lilian Audrey. We discovered that she died in 1985 and that the death was recorded at Nottingham. I obtained a copy of the death certificate from the Registrar, and I attach a photocopy. As you will see from this, she took her own life at the age of 53 and this death certificate in many ways has raised more questions than it has answered. For example, where did she drown, who identified the body, where was she buried/cremated, and is there any memorial for her? Also, were the Police involved and are we entitled to know anything about their enquiries?*
>
> *The discovery that my mother ended her own life has been a shock, but after consideration I feel that it is worse being in ignorance of the facts than knowing them and coming to terms with it. I hope you will be able to help me.*

I had expressed my fears that Audrey (Mary) was already dead to both Aunt Joan and my sister Jill. Now I had to confirm that those fears were founded and the manner of her death. Both were saddened, of course, but not unduly surprised. In a way, it solved a problem. Jill was still not sure if she wanted to meet her birth mother. Margaret, her adoptive mother, had sadly died a few years previously, so one of the original constraints had been removed, but Jill was still undecided what she wanted to do if Audrey was traced. It would have been rather difficult for me to re-establish a relationship with my mother without ever mentioning that I was in contact with my sister and her adopted daughter, Jill. However, that awkward situation would now never arise.

It was also necessary for us to inform Joan's solicitor that it had now been established that Audrey, the youngest sibling, was dead and so would never be traced. The solicitor had contacted John Green some months previously and informed him that Joan had found Audrey's daughters and that efforts were underway to trace Audrey herself and had reiterated Joan's wish that she and John jointly return a third of Dorothy's estate for the benefit of Audrey or her daughters, even though there was no legal obligation to do so due to Audrey's adoption. John had written a very wordy reply dated July 2, 2001, but for the purposes of this narrative, the significant paragraph stated:-

"I may be prepared voluntarily and not under duress to put aside £60,000 of my inheritance for the benefit of Mary provided that if she is not alive or not traced then to a registered charity or charities of my own choosing - and provided Joan does likewise..."

John had said that, in the event of Mary's (Audrey's) death, he would be prepared to put aside a third of his inheritance for charity. Once he knew the full circumstances of his youngest sister's life, particularly what a sham her adoption had been, her mental illness, the breakdown of her marriage and how all this had impacted on her daughters, would he be prepared to consider giving the £60,000 for the benefit of his nieces instead? Joan felt passionately that he should. I therefore helped Joan to pen a letter to be sent to John via her solicitor, setting these further facts before him. It said, in part:-

In May of this year, I succeeded in tracing our nieces, Julie and Jill. They joined with me in trying to find (their mother). Sadly, we have just received confirmation that Lilian Audrey Goodwin died in 1985. A copy of the death certificate is attached.

I am fully aware that, due to being adopted, our youngest sister, Lilian Audrey Goodwin nee Gladys Mary Green, and her children, our nieces, have no legal claim under Dorothy's estate. However, I would like to point out that Gladys Mary grew up with us in the orphanage, not being adopted until she was 13 years of age. It was at her adoption in 1945 that her name was changed from Gladys Mary Green to Lilian Audrey Freeman. She was not happy with the couple she was placed with; in fact she claimed that her adoptive father sexually abused her. Not surprisingly, therefore, by 1947 she had left them and was living with me in lodging rooms. She and Dorothy were bridesmaids at my wedding in December 1949, and Dorothy and I attended her wedding in 1951. I believe, being adopted at such a late stage, and in view of the abuse she claimed she suffered, she never viewed them as parents nor kept in contact with them. In fact, on her marriage certificate to Herbert Goodwin in 1972, she has cited our father Edward Green, rather than her adoptive parent William Arthur Freeman, as her father.

Due to these sad circumstances and other very harrowing details of Lilian Audrey's life, which John cannot possibly be aware of as he did not keep in touch with us, had I succeeded in finding our youngest sister alive I would certainly have wanted her to benefit under Dorothy's estate. I therefore propose, now that we can be certain of our sister's untimely death at the age of 53, that my brother and I should voluntarily and not under duress gift £60,000 each to her daughters, (who after all are his nieces as well as mine), to be shared equally between them.

This combined £120,000 would, in effect, constitute approximately one-third of Dorothy's estate.

I particularly want to say that I am very pleased to have found my two nieces, Julie and Jill, and that they are both

> *very clever girls, in my opinion, so I am very proud of them. They have been very kind to me, and I am happy to be in touch with family who can comfort and support me, particularly in view of the recently received sad news about Lilian Audrey…*

Meanwhile, within a few days of receiving my letter, Dr. Nigel Chapman, the Nottinghamshire Coroner, rang me personally to tell me that they had located my mother's inquest report in their archives and that I could come to his offices to look through it if I was sure that is what I wanted. I was to contact his secretary to make an appointment.

On the appointed date, I took the afternoon off work because I wasn't sure how reading details about my mother's death would affect me. I arrived at the coroner's offices, made myself known, and was ushered into a private room. Dr. Chapman brought the file to me. I was told that I could take my time over reading it, but that I should not make any notes or take anything away. There were some private (suicide) notes which my mother had written, and I could take these away with me if I wished. I was assured that an announcement had been placed in the Nottingham Evening Post shortly after her death, in the hopes that any relatives would come forward, but to no avail.

Once I was alone, I began to read through the file. It was very concise. As I was not allowed to take any notes, I do not remember all the details, but certain things I remember very well.

From the police statements, it appears that on June 10, 1985, a man and a woman had been walking their dog late at night along the River Trent embankment near Trent Bridge when they passed a woman walking in the opposite direction. Her clothing was described in detail, but all I can remember was that she was wearing a headscarf. My mother had often worn a headscarf.

A short time later, they heard a splash, looked around, and the woman had disappeared. They spotted what looked like a bundle of clothes in the water, travelling downstream. They ran alongside the River until the "bundle" floated near enough the bank of the river to be retrieved, upon which it became apparent that, as they feared, it was the woman they had passed earlier. An ambulance was summoned and attempts were made to resuscitate the woman before she was rushed to Queen's Medical Centre where she was pronounced dead on arrival.

In the meantime, the police had called Audrey's flat at 6 Half Moon Drive, Kirkby-in-Ashfield. They had been asked to call on several occasions recently because Audrey claimed that the neighbours upstairs were making a dreadful noise into the early hours of the morning. She had not been able to sleep. Her husband Herbert had died nine months previously. Had these problems with the neighbours been happening before he died, or had they started since? It is impossible for me to say, but it is apparent that now Herbert was no longer around to support her, Audrey was not coping very well with the situation.

She had left a note for the police, stating her intentions, and had also pushed a note through the neighbour's letterbox before, presumably, taking a bus or a taxi from Kirkby-in-Ashfield to Trent Bridge on the outskirts of Nottingham city centre.

The autopsy took place on June 19. The coroner noted in his report the faint, telltale scars on Audrey's forehead, which indicated an earlier leucotomy (lobotomy) and concluded that this woman had evidently suffered from severe mental illness. Comment was also made regarding her nicely manicured hands and nails. Certain internal organs had been removed and their weight noted.

At this point a woman popped her head around the door and inquired if I was all right. I assured her that I was. I felt that everyone knew in advance that I was coming and why and was expecting me to be very emotional, maybe even distraught. Perhaps I disappointed them and appeared hard and unfeeling. However, I felt only numbness as I thumbed through the pages of the coroner's report. It seemed almost surreal, as though I was in no way connected to the person I was reading about. I don't like showing emotion publicly and felt that some sort of safety valve had shut down my feelings for the day, making it impossible for me to shed any tears, although many were shed before and have been since.

On my departure, Dr. Chapman asked me if I would like to take the private notes which my mother had written away with me. I declined his offer. Before catching the bus home, I called at the County Library on Angel Row and asked to see the micro-fiche of the *Nottingham Evening Post* where my mother's death had been reported. After some searching, I found it reported after the account of another drowning. It read:

> *"Meanwhile, the body of a woman found in the River Trent on Monday evening has been identified as that of Lillian Audrey Goodwin, 53, of Half Moon Drive, Kirkby. Nottinghamshire Coroner Mr. John Langham is appealing for relatives, or any person who can give any information on the dead woman, to contact the coroner's office...An inquest will be opened next week."*

I used to buy the *Evening Post* maybe twice a week. It's possible I may even have bought this particular issue, but I only skimmed through it so it's unlikely I would have noticed these few lines. One of my father's sisters may well have read it, but they wouldn't have known Audrey's surname after her second marriage, Goodwin, so it wouldn't have meant anything to them. Some weeks later, I changed my mind about my mother's private notes and wrote to Dr. Chapman, asking if I may still have them. He forwarded them on to me. I have probably only read them twice, but I feel that now they are where they belong, with me, rather than in a forgotten file gathering dust in the coroner's archives. The most coherent note reads:-

> *The people in the (top) flat drove me to this. They would not give me any kind of peace. They kept me awake all night. I am sorry to have been driven to this. Stephen (Policeman?) will confirm what I have written. I had a good husband, but he did not cause it. I am sorry but I hope it will kill me so I can get some rest. I think God will understand. I don't think I have anything else to tell you. Mrs. Goodwin*

My visit to see the coroner's report into my mother's death had answered most of the questions I had, which were, Where did she drown? Who identified the body? Were the police involved, and was I entitled to know anything about their inquiries?

I felt relieved that her body had not been in the water for an extended period of time. I was pleased that it had been recovered less than half an hour after she jumped in, and before it became bloated and partially decomposed.

However, a fourth question was, where was she buried or cremated, and is there any memorial for her? The coroner told me that the funeral had been dealt with by Mansfield Crematorium. I therefore telephoned them and spoke to the cemetery officer, Lynne Cooper. She was able to confirm that my mother had been cremated there in June 1985, and a Mr. Richard Malcolm Massey had been in attendance at the funeral and signed the necessary documentation.

I wondered if this gentleman might be related to Herbert, Audrey's second husband—a nephew, perhaps? I looked in the Mansfield telephone directory to try to find his telephone number, and it was listed! I therefore wrote to him, briefly explaining the circumstances of my mother's death and asking what connection he had with her. The following morning, Mr. Massey telephoned me. However, he regretted informing me that he had merely been an employee of Ashfield District Council at the time. No friends or relations having come forward in answer to the notice placed in the *Evening Post*, the responsibility to arrange Audrey's funeral had fallen on the local council. Mr. Massey had been at the funeral as the council's official representative, not as anyone connected with my mother. Had anyone mourned her passing? It seemed not, until now. A few weeks after my visit to the coroner's office, I found I just could not carry on at work any longer and had to take a fortnight off. I was engulfed with feelings of anger, guilt, and sadness over what had happened to my mother. I had so many regrets, so many unanswered questions which, had she still been alive, I would have been able to ask her.

During the time I was off work, I tried to get my thoughts into some kind of order, to reach acceptance and closure, to move on. I hope that writing this book will help me to settle within myself some unresolved issues, to forgive myself, and to defend my mother's reputation, for I can honestly say that in all my life up until meeting Aunt Joan, I only heard her spoken of disparagingly. Maybe knowing the truth about her childhood would help my father's family in particular to think of her more kindly.

During her fifty-three years of life, it seems to me my mother was always a victim. A victim of circumstances due to the death of her mother, a victim of the culture of the time, where no provision was made for fathers to stay at home to care for their children, leaving no alternative but to hand them over to the care of an institution. Adopted at thirteen years of age, not because it was in her best interests, but because, I now have reason to believe, it was expedient for others. Married to my father at twenty years of age, she had a complete mental breakdown immediately after my birth from which she never fully recovered. In desperation, she accepted an irreversible brain operation (leucotomy/ lobotomy), which robbed her of her true personality, therefore becoming a victim of a medical "fad" of the time.

Misunderstood and reviled by her husband's family, who never had a good word to say about her. Forced, due to her mental illness, to give a second daughter up for adoption, she later suffered rejection by the child she was able to keep. Yet I have come to know that, in the final fourteen years of her life, my mother had something which perhaps few of us ever give or receive in our lifetime - unconditional love. Herbert Goodwin, the fifty-seven-year-old widower who married my mother and who I regarded as a pathetic old man when I met him as a self-assured seventeen-year-old, accepted and loved my mother despite her past, despite her limitations, purely and simply for who and what she was. Her suicide note indicates that she was happy with him, that he had been "a good husband." This is of immeasurable comfort to me. I resolved to place an entry for my mother in the Book of Remembrance at Mansfield Crematorium. Many months passed before I finally decided on the citation to use:-

GOODWIN, Lilian Audrey: Born Gladys Mary Green, 1931

"He will take pity on the weak and the needy, the afflicted who have no-one to help" Psalm 72: verses 12 & 13

CHAPTER 6
The Children's Homes, Beeston

MY EARLIER EFFORTS TO FIND out more information regarding the Children's Homes where my mother grew up had been very disappointing. I had so many unanswered questions, which I would have asked her personally, had she still been alive. Now I felt I must find out as much as I possibly could, as a sort of penance, I suppose, for my previous disinterest. I therefore renewed my efforts, writing to various agencies in an attempt to learn more. However, it transpired that even the Social Services and Adoption Agencies knew very little about this institution.

I learned that the Nottingham Archives had committee meeting minutes for the Beeston Children's Homes dating way back to the 1880s, but the particular period I was interested in—when my mother, her sisters, and brother were living there—was in a closure period until January 2016. However, at my request, the Social Services Department of Nottingham County Council arranged for an investigative officer to visit the archives and access the committee meeting minutes on my behalf, reporting back to me any mention of my relatives. I hoped that these minutes would shed some light on a question which had increasingly been troubling me. That question was, Why had my mother been adopted at thirteen years of age, just five months before she was due to leave school, and had her father, who was still alive at the time, authorized the adoption?

When the investigative officer reported back to me, his findings were most disappointing. He stated that "the minutes are recorded monthly and only mention the names of children admitted and discharged. It was clear that they were not all recorded. The Homes held fifty children and over the period I looked at (1930–1946) only about forty names were recorded."

However, there had been mention of Joan, Dorothy, John, and Mary Green. They were recorded as being admitted to the Homes on October 1, 1937. I questioned this immediately. Their mother had died in 1933, and Joan had stated that their father had placed them in the care of the Homes shortly afterwards. How could the minutes be correct in stating, therefore, that they had not been admitted until 1937? The investigative officer suggested that Joan's recollection of events was probably defective. After all, she was an elderly lady.

In stark contrast with the lack of important details given in regard to the admission and discharge of most of the children, it was recorded in the minutes that on April 14, 1942, John Green left the Homes to go and work in an office. He had twelve shillings pocket money and four National Savings Certificates. His patron? Mr. George Thornton Simpson, a partner in the firm of Messrs. Acton, Marriott, and Simpson, Solicitors. Mr. Simpson had been a trustee of the Beeston Children's Homes since 1922 and was the chairperson of the committee.

The matter of the date of the children's admittance to the Homes concerned me. If I accepted what was recorded in the committee meeting minutes, it meant that my mother had been six years of age when they were admitted to the Homes, yet she was only a babe in arms when her mother died. Who had cared for her all that time? It just didn't add up.

I had an idea. The school admissions records for many Beeston schools were also housed at the Nottingham Archives, and these were then open to the public. (Sadly, these records have now been closed to the public under the Data Protection Act.) I asked to see records for the infant school, which was situated on Church Street. Dorothy and John Green are clearly shown as having been admitted to the school in September 1933, four months (not four years), after their mother died. Their address is given as the orphanage at Beeston. My mother Mary was later admitted to the same school in September 1936, at five years of age, and her address is also noted as the Orphanage, Beeston. I felt vindicated and concluded that the committee meeting minutes of the Children's Homes could not necessarily be depended on as a reliable source of information.

Frustrated with the poor results my inquiries to various agencies were yielding, I decided to try an altogether different approach. One social worker had informed me that the Children's Homes had later become known as "Silverwood Hall." I therefore wrote to the

Replies to Readers column in the *Nottingham Evening Post* and asked the question, "Does anyone have any information about, or memories of, Silverwood Hall Orphanage in Beeston, particularly in the 1930s and '40s?" (I later learned that the Children's Homes only became known as Silverwood Hall after they were transferred to the Nottingham Corporation in 1947.) This column in the *Evening Post* was run by a lady called Maureen Humberston. After a few weeks, I received an envelope in the mail, and enclosed were three replies which Maureen had received to my query.

I read them all with interest. One was from a gentleman called Mr. Hall, and his reply was also later printed in the Replies to Readers column in the *Evening Post*. It read:

> *In the Summer of 1960, the orphanage was undergoing a revamp. I was laying floor covering and was doing the work on my own. The rooms were very small and there was a mass of small staircases and landings. One Friday evening I locked up and went home to Attenborough and realized I had left some tools. As I needed them for the weekend, I went back with my two-year-old daughter to pick them up. On unlocking the door my daughter wanted to know why the little boy was crying. (I still get goose flesh writing this.)*
>
> *I told her there was no one there, but she was insistent and said he was upstairs crying. She took me to the room, and we went in. There was no one there, but she was very upset and said: "He's still crying." We then left the building.*
>
> *I went back on Monday to the room, and for some unknown reason, I took some floorboards up and found an old Victorian wooden train.*
>
> *I knew an old gent who lived on Imperial Road, and he told me that in the old days, a gentleman would ride up Imperial Road on a white horse and inspect the orphans in the courtyard. They stood barefoot in all weathers.*
>
> *I went back to Silverwood about three months later to do some repairs and asked the lady who was running the place how she liked living there. She told me it wasn't too bad, but it's spooky.*

The second was a letter from a gentleman called Sydney Metcalf. He wrote:-

> *Regarding an Orphanage at Beeston, the only one that I know was the one on the Imperial Road where the buses used to terminate at the bottom. My brother and I and our family were there. I am a twin and we started work in that Orphanage, in short trousers, working at Ericsons, early '40s.*

The last, but by no means the least letter was from a lady called Olwen Reddish. She wrote:-

Dear Maureen

Re. Your enquiry in the Evening Post—memories of Silverwood House, Beeston. Would you mind telling me what you wish to know, maybe I can help! No visits please, only by appointment, because of disablement.

Hoping to hear from you.

I didn't respond to Mr. Hall's reply, as although it was interesting, it related to the early 1960s, not the period I was interested in. After the Nottingham City Council took over the Children's Homes in 1947, they used them as a hostel for maladjusted boys with severe behavioral problems for around a decade, and then as accommodation for university students. The work Mr. Hall was doing was in relation to the conversion of the building to student accommodation in the late 1950s/early 1960s.

I rang Sydney Metcalf because he and his family had clearly been resident at the Homes at the same time as my mother and her older brother and sisters. We had a lengthy conversation on the telephone and then Sydney kindly agreed to my request to pay him a visit at his home to continue our discussion.

I then rang Olwen Reddish. She told me that she had been resident at the Homes from 1929, when she was seven years old, to 1946, when she left to get married. Her mother had been the matron. I told her that relatives of mine had been admitted to the Homes in 1933. They were Joan, Dorothy, John, and Mary Green. Mary was my mother. Did she remember them? Olwen told me that, in general, she had very little to do with the other children who lived in the Homes, although she was only about three years older than my Aunt Joan, so would have been ten or eleven when the Greens were admitted.

I decided not to mention anything negative about my mother's life or her tragic death. I simply stated that she had been adopted at thirteen years of age by a couple called Freeman who lived on Imperial Road, the same street as the Homes.

"Yes, I knew them," Olwen confessed.

Intrigued, I continued talking, telling her how Dorothy had become a teacher and John a member of the legal profession, despite their disadvantaged start in life. However, I sensed that Olwen was "closing up." She had been quite guarded from the beginning of our conversation, but now I felt that she had definitely put up a barrier, although she had expressed a willingness to give information about the Homes in her reply to Maureen Humberston of the *Evening Post*, even saying that she would be prepared for someone to call if they made an appointment beforehand.

I tried to continue the conversation in a cheery way, hoping she would invite me to pay her a visit, but she had obviously decided against this. Just before the call drew to a close, I asked her, "What was your mother's name?"

"Freeman," came the reply.

"Oh, any relation to the couple who adopted my mother, or is that just a coincidence?"

"Oh no, no relation at all."

Our telephone conversation ended, leaving me very frustrated. Here was someone who had lived at the Homes for seventeen years. She knew the people who had adopted my mother. I wanted to ask her so many questions, but the feeling that she had put up a barrier for whatever reason prevented me from doing so. Could I possibly be imagining or misreading the situation? It was difficult to tell as we were total strangers talking for the first time over the telephone, not face-to-face.

I decided to give her the benefit of the doubt and wrote to Olwen Reddish, hoping that my letter would encourage her to be more forthcoming. It read:-

26 October 2001

Dear Mrs. Reddish

I would like to thank you for responding to my question in the Evening Post about memories of Silverwood Hall (Old Beeston Orphanage). As you lived there between 1929–46, you certainly should be able to recall quite a lot about the place!

As I think I told you on the telephone, my mother, two aunts and an uncle, the Greens, lived at the Orphanage from 1933 after the tragic death of their mother.

It is my intention to write a book about my family history and obviously the Orphanage will feature in this. I wish to give as accurate an account as possible and am therefore doing quite a lot of research before I write anything. Through the Evening Post, I have been able to contact five children (in addition to my family) who were living at the Orphanage about the time my relations were there. They have noted down their recollections on the enclosed form. However, I wish to get a rounded-out picture, and would therefore value your reminiscences, if you are prepared to share them. When you have had time to consider this, please write or telephone me, and I will be pleased to arrange to visit you at a time convenient to yourself. Or, if you would rather I didn't visit you, perhaps you would prefer to jot down a few lines and send them through the mail.

I would be very appreciative of any information you could give me. I hope that my book, when I eventually write it, will not only be of interest to me because it involves my family, but will also be a valuable piece of social history.

I never received a reply.

Happily, Sydney Metcalf was far more agreeable to sharing his recollections of life at the Children's Homes with me. When I visited Sydney and his wife Mary, they made me very welcome, and I immediately felt at ease with them. I had prepared a questionnaire, which I hoped would serve as a memory jogger, as I was asking people to delve back in their minds almost fifty-five years. Whilst Sydney's wife Mary made us a cup of tea, Sydney handed me a cutting from a newspaper (believed to be the *Nottingham Evening Post*), which explained the circumstances that led to him being admitted to the Homes along with his twin David, his other brother Frank, and three sisters, Pearl, Hedera, and Violet. It was dated April 8, 1938, and began:-

SIX CHILDREN LEFT MOTHERLESS
BRAMCOTE WOMAN KILLED BY HEAVY LORRY
INQUEST AT BEESTON

"ACCIDENTAL DEATH" was the verdict which the jury returned at an inquest held at the Town Hall, Beeston, on Monday afternoon, concerning the death of Mrs. Ivy Elizabeth Metcalf of 97 Cow Lane, Bramcote, Nottingham.

Mrs. Metcalf, who was thirty-two years of age, was killed while riding a pedal cycle, which came into collision with a petrol tank lorry at the junction of Derby Road and Wollaton Road, Beeston, last Saturday morning.

In returning their verdict, the jury exonerated the driver of the lorry from blame expressing the belief that he took all precautions. Evidence was given by Squire Priest Metcalf, husband of Mrs. Metcalf. This witness said that his wife was the mother of six children and was in good health. Her eyesight and hearing were good..."

I tried to visualize Derby Road, now the main A52 link road between Derby and Nottingham, a dual carriageway with three lanes either side, as it would have been in 1938. There was probably very little other traffic on the road. Mrs. Metcalf 's daughter Pearl confirms that her mother was cycling to work, a journey she had made many, many times before without coming to any harm. This time there were fatal consequences, and the lives of six children would never be the same again.

Sydney explained that his mother had originally been Squire Priest Metcalf 's housekeeper. He and his brother David became the stepsons of Mr. Metcalf when he married their mother. Mrs. Metcalf went on to have four more children, another boy, Frank, and three girls, Pearl, Hedera, and Violet. Finding himself unable to cope with this large family following his wife's tragic death, Mr. Metcalf was advised to put them in the care of the Homes, and he paid toward their upkeep. Sydney had already taken the time to write down as much as he could remember about the daily routine of life in the Children's Homes. Here are his recollections as he wrote them, but anything in brackets I have added.

Mrs Lovatt (actually Florence May Lovelock) taken ill and died on 11 July 1940. Taken over by Mrs Freeman. Up in the morning, getting washed and dressed. Prayers was said always the same, starting, 'We thank thee Lord for this our food'. Anywhere we were always in twos. The girls went to Nether Street School.

"Up in the morning, getting washed and dressed, then as the older boys had to look after one young one, had to wash and dress them, make all beds, and Ronuck [a sort of all-purpose polish] and clean all bedrooms before breakfast, then line up in twos in the corridor to march into the room for breakfast."

Prayers was said always the same starting, "We thank thee, Lord, for this our food." Children under 12 years had two slices of bread, and children over 12 years had 3 slices of bread, which was covered in syrup the night before. This was to us the best meal and was always looked for. Alternatively, it would be lumpy porridge. Dinner was mostly liver and onions followed by suet pudding.

The lady in charge of the girls was Mrs. or Miss McCready, who nobody liked. The spending money was 2p a week in old money. The girls did the laundry and vegetables for meals. When old enough to leave the home, if not returning home, they would be put into service.

As regards the boys, before we went to school, all our shoes were checked to see that we had thirteen studs and that they were highly polished, and the ribs of our socks had to be straight, and returning they were always checked. Then after dinner all downstairs had to be cleaned with Ronuck and highly polished before bedtime.

The only time we ever went out was once every year to the Nottingham Pantomime. The only other time we were allowed out was going to all choir practices, which was three times a week, as the choir was made up from the Orphanage, and Sunday school, and every church service, the church being Beeston Parish Church. The choirmaster was Mr. Alton. This can be verified from the church records.

Having reached the age of 14, those that did not go back home was sent to places like Australia or New Zealand, but I was fortunate that I was returning back home. [When I questioned Sydney later and asked if he could remember any children who were actually sent abroad as child migrants, he said that he couldn't.]

While waiting, I started work from the Orphanage in short trousers, working at Ericsons, Beeston. Talk about being out of place, but we was accepted, my brother and I, as we are twins. Incidentally, the only birthday party to be held at the home was for us twins.

Whenever we came back, wherever we went, on returning, all our clothes had to be brushed and folded and put away. It was strict but looking back stood us all in good stead for future years in life. No machines at all, everything done by hand!

Sorry I cannot remember much more...

-Sydney Metcalf

Sydney was born in 1926 and was eleven years old when he went to live at the Children's Homes. He stayed until 1941. I asked him what his happiest memory was during that time, and he said it was going to the pantomime at the Theatre Royal at Christmas time. When asked if he had a particularly unhappy memory, he said that Mrs. Hallam, nicknamed "The Gorilla," used to scrub you until raw on bath night, which was once a week, with carbolic soap and a hard scrubbing brush. He could not remember any of my relatives, the Greens.

As we sat drinking our tea, I thought what a devoted couple Sydney and Mary were. They had been married for forty-three years and had one daughter and a grandson.

Sydney told me that, sadly, his brother Frank had been killed in a brawl in Germany in the 1990s. However, he gave me the addresses of his twin brother David, who lived in South Africa and his three sisters. Pearl lived in Tasmania, Violet and Hedera both lived in Wales. I forwarded a letter and copy of my questionnaire to these other family members.

Although my initial interest in the Children's Homes sprang from a personal desire to learn about my mother's childhood, I became convinced that the information I was collating was also an important piece of social history.

Before the Children's Act 1948, when the local authorities became more responsible for children in care, there were hundreds of these privately run charitable institutions across the country. The treatment of the children in these Homes would not be considered acceptable today. However, was there any preferable alternative at the time?

CHAPTER 7
The Children Remember

FOLLOWING MY VISIT TO SYDNEY Metcalf, all three of his sisters— Violet, Pearl, and Hedera—returned the questionnaire I had posted out to them. Their brother David in South Africa did not reply, but Sydney had warned me he probably wouldn't. David had always thought it best to put this period in his life behind him, preferring not to dwell on their time in the Beeston Children's Homes.

Here is the questionnaire as completed by Violet:

**MEMORIES OF THE OLD
BEESTON ORPHANAGE**

Your Name: Violet (nee Metcalf)

Year of Birth: 1931

Address: Supplied

Tel. No: Supplied

If you can remember, please state how old you were
when you went to live at the Beeston Children's Home?

7 yrs. 7 months

How old were you when you left?

12

Would you consider your time spent there was…
Happy   Unhappy   A bit of both - (No answer given)

Can you recall a HAPPY memory?

Not one. Although we were unhappy, we were fed, clothed and kept warm. I do remember coming back from school in winter with feet so cold they were white. We wore laced ankle boots.

Can you recall an UNHAPPY memory?

Being invited by a school friend to see A Midsummer Night's Dream. The older sister used the name "Vera" instead of Violet. My sister Pearl was sent instead.

Mary and I drew something silly on the Blackboard. Mary went with the others to see a film. I wasn't allowed to go. If Mrs. Freeman couldn't find out who had done something wrong, I usually received the punishment.

Do you remember any of these people? (Please tick answer)

Ms. Lovelock
Mrs. Hallam
Mrs. Freeman

Ms. MacCready - (added by Violet)
Do you have any specific memories about them?

Ms. Lovelock very little but never remember her ever being unpleasant.

Mrs. Hallam we girls saw very little of.
Mrs. Freeman had a great dislike for we three sisters. I don't remember ever having a kind word from her.
Ms. MacCready, I found gentle and helpful although I know Hedera has quite different memories.

Do you recall anyone else involved in your care or the running of the orphanage?

Mrs. Freeman's daughter Olwen was often very helpful.
Mrs. Alton (spelling?) did sew and mending.
Mr. Alton should not have been near children.

Do you remember any of the Following children?

Joan Caroline Green (born 1925)
Dorothy Olive Green (born 1926)
John Edwin Green (born 1928)
Gladys Mary Green (born 1931)

Do you remember anything specifically about them?

Mary had quite dark skin on her neck. Mrs.
Freeman used a scrubbing brush on her neck
and was surprised that the skin remained dark.
Could John have been the boy with the
lovely singing voice that sang Jerusalem
at one of the concerts we gave?

Do you remember any other children by name?

Marion Clark
Margaret and Freddie Smith
Brenda Mann
Priscilla and Helena (can't remember the surname)
Leslie with the ginger hair who frequently wet
his bed. He was embarrassed in front of the
whole dining room. Leslie once had the wet sheet
wrapped round his neck during breakfast. This
was Mrs. Freeman's doing, not Mrs. Hallam.

**Which school did you attend whilst at
the Beeston Children's Home?**

Church St. Junior
Nether Street Senior. During the war went to half-day school
but can't recall where it was.

**Were the Orphanage children treated
any differently at school?**

As far as I know, we were not except by one

teacher at the half-day school. Whether it was just me or whether because I was a "Charity Kid," I never knew. She was hateful.

Thank you for sharing your memories

The following notes were written on the back of the questionnaire:-
Some memories remain very clear:-

Breakfast: Four mornings a week porridge. Three mornings half slice of bread and syrup.
Dinners: Mainly stew with rice pudding to follow. I was once forced to swallow three pieces of fat and was immediately sick...

Tea: One slice of bread and jam, two days a week we had a piece of cake. I don't ever remember being hungry.

Before making our beds in the morning, holding our sheets up to the light to make sure they were not stained.

Top right of the blue door, matron's bedroom. Top left was the sickroom. Bottom right was the playroom. Bottom left the dining room. Bottom extreme left staff sitting room. Extreme right on the bottom, sewing room.

Later, Violet wrote to me again and enclosed two photographs of the Children's Homes before they were demolished. I greatly appreciated these, as I had been unable to obtain a single photograph of the Children's Homes, although I had approached Beeston Historical Society and scoured publications of Beeston in times past.

Violet's letter reads, in part: "It is very puzzling that there seems to be so little information about the orphanage, as you say it was there for many years. This snap was taken in 1986. The family are my daughter and her children, which makes it easy to date the picture."

The three Green sisters at the Children's Home: Mary, second row back, first on the left. Dorothy, second row back, third from the left. Joan is the row behind, fourth from the left. This picture was taken circa 1934/35 before the Metcalfe sisters arrived.

"From what I remember of Mary, she was quite a timid child. It is impossible for anyone to understand what goes through the human brain. If you have never been loved, how can you know what love is? Many think love is a natural human emotion. It is not. To be able to love you first have to be loved. When a man falls in love with a woman who has never known love, as I know only too well, you just can't believe that someone actually loves you and wants to marry you and you think how wonderful life is going to be. It doesn't work out so simply. The woman needs treating gently and has to be taught how to love and that is asking too much of any man because he won't understand. My second child gave me some understanding of love."

"It took my husband's family a very long time to really accept me. Those of us brought up in 'homes' are never quite like other people. Try as I might to be like others, I'm not. Missing out on family life when young make you different, which is most unfortunate."

I greatly appreciated hearing from Violet because she actually remembered my mother, Mary Green, very well. They had been good friends.

Hedera had also filled in and returned the questionnaire with a brief letter which said, in part:

"I'm sorry I can't be much help about the orphanage, but maybe Violet or Pearl might remember more. I'm afraid I really hated being there. I couldn't wait for the day to come for me to leave…

"I hope you have some luck in writing your book. I shall be very interested in reading what you have written. If I think of anything at all, I will let you know.

"I can remember the German planes overhead fighting when we were going over to the air raid shelter…"

Here is Hedera's completed questionnaire:

MEMORIES OF THE OLD BEESTON ORPHANAGE

Your Name: Hedera (nee Metcalfe)

Year of Birth: 1928

Address: Supplied

Tel. No: Supplied

If you can remember, how old you were when you went to live at the Beeston Children's Home? - 10 years

How old were you when you left? - 14 years

Would you consider your time spent there was… (Tick the answer.) Happy/Unhappy/ A bit of both
Can you recall a HAPPY memory?

Ms. McCready dressed a doll, with yellow dress and bonnet whilst I was in hospital and gave it to me, from her and the girls. Unfortunately, I wasn't able to take it with me when I returned. (I was 8 months in hospital as I was a diphtheria carrier.)

Can you recall an UNHAPPY memory?

I was sent to the Pantomime instead of my sister Violet with her friend's family. Mrs. Freeman didn't seem to like Violet. I was most unhappy about this as it hurt Violet.

Do you remember any of these people? (Please tick answer.)

Ms. Lovelock
Mrs. Hallam
Mrs. Freeman

Do you have any specific memories about them?

Ms. Lovelock snatched our toffee wrappers and threw them away. When I burst into tears, she retrieved mine with the uneaten bit in it.

Ms. Hallam - never forgot how she ate her toast. Cut up small, two chews, and a swallow! Pleasant lady.

Mrs. Freeman—Being smacked three times on each hand with a sand shoe because I cried, another three on my bottom in front of other inmates who were cleaning. The offence was a 1½–3-inch urine stain on my sheet.
Do you recall anyone else involved in your care or the running of the orphanage?

Ms. McCready cared for me when I had mumps and measles. Was preparing me for confirmation just before I left. Her Bible teaching wasn't wasted. She always had time for us, a lovely lady.

Mr. Arnold—he had twin sons.

Do you remember any of the following children? (Please tick.)

Joan Caroline Green (born 1925)
Dorothy Olive Green (born 1926)
John Edwin Green (born 1928)
Gladys Mary Green (born 1931)

Do you remember anything specifically about them?

Mary, as we knew her, was a nice girl but
could never do any wrong so far as Mrs.
Freeman went. Always had a smile, she wore
glasses if my memory is correct. I didn't have
much to do with her, but I liked her.

Do you remember any other children by name?

Fred and Margaret Smith (Fred wore glasses)
Helen and Priscilla (surname?)
Kenneth with a leg iron on one leg
Phillip and elder brother Leslie

Which school did you attend whilst at
the Beeston Children's Home?

Roundhill Primary. 1st and 4th years sick
so missed 2 years Junior School.

Were the Orphanage children treated
any differently at school?

The only time I recall was during a very heavy
Snowfall in 1941/42. We were not sent to school
And the headmistress ridiculed us the next
day for not going. I don't recall any treatment
from staff or students other than that.

Thank you for sharing your memories.

Due to the kindness of the Metcalf family, I was finally able to begin building up a picture of what life in the Children's Homes had been like for my mother, who spent almost her entire childhood there. They spoke frankly, openly, and from first-hand experience, which I felt was far more true to life than any account a local historian could have compiled.

Some months later, on May 7, 2002, Sydney Metcalf rang me to say that there was an article in that night's *Nottingham Evening Post* about Brenda Robinson, nee Mann, who had also spent some years in the Beeston Children's Homes. Whilst there, she attended Church Street Junior School and Nether Street Girls' School and had become great friends with another girl called Irene. The two school friends lost contact with each other in 1946 when Brenda left the orphanage to return home. Now, fifty-six years later, they were both by chance members of the same church choir but didn't recognize each other for two years! Then, they happened to sit together at the choir's annual dinner and got talking. Brenda mentioned that she had been brought up in the Children's Homes on Imperial Road, which jolted Irene's memory and made her realize that Brenda was actually her long lost school friend! They were delighted to be reunited again.

The *Evening Post* article ended with an appeal from Brenda, saying that she would like to hear from other people who were in the orphanage from 1930–1946 and giving her telephone number. I immediately contacted Brenda and was invited to visit her home and discuss my family's history.

Brenda is a very warm and outgoing lady and spoke of her time in the Children's Homes more positively than any of the others I had interviewed. Her father had died, and as her mother had to work, she left Brenda and her brother Gordon in the care of the Homes.

Brenda was born in 1934. She came to live at the Children's Homes in 1939, at four years of age and left in 1946 at eleven years of age. Her elder brother Gordon was there from 1939 to 1943.

In 1946, Brenda returned to live with her mother permanently. The only explanation she could give for this was that the Homes were "closing down". This agreed with what Violet Metcalf had told me when I said that I was puzzled as to the reasons for my mother's adoption at thirteen years of age. She said the reason for it was likely that the Homes were closing down. In fact, they did not close down but were taken over by the Nottingham Corporation.

Brenda has given talks at various local venues about her time in the Children's Homes. When the Homes were completely demolished, a nursing home called Silverwood was erected on the site. After seeing the article about Brenda in the *Nottingham Evening Post*, the proprietors asked her to attend the Queen's Golden Jubilee celebrations at the nursing home in 2002 and give a talk about the time she spent there when it was an orphanage.

During my visit, she also talked animatedly about her memories of life in the Old Beeston Orphanage, as follows:-

"My first memory is a member of staff carrying me around the girl's playroom as I was crying for my mother.

"The layout of this huge Victorian building was boys one end and girls the other. A corridor ran the length of the home with a door kept closed in the middle except for mealtimes. Before each meal, there would be two bells: the first hurry up and get into line, little ones in front, with arms folded behind our backs. We'd march into the cloakroom/washroom, which was a very sparse room. There was a row of wash basins, two toilets for about twenty girls and metal cupboards for coats and one to accommodate all the lace-up boots. The second bell meant we could walk into the dining room and stand behind our forms at the long tables covered with white oil cloth. Then the boys would come into their tables at the other side of the room and then I would see the smiling face of my big brother. "Matron would come in wearing a white organza square head-dress, followed by the staff, and sit at the oval table covered by a white damask linen cloth. She would say grace, tell us to sit and eat, children no talking. When finished again, we'd fold our arms behind our back. Generally speaking, we had good substantial meals. The war started September 1939, but we didn't know much about it, as we never heard a radio or saw a paper. We had gas masks, and if the sirens went in the night, we had blue siren suits—the boys had brown—and we went into the corridor and laid on the floor each resting your head on the next one's hips in a long line.

"We had normal schooling. I didn't seem to be treated any different from others in class. I do remember crying with cold feet and chilblains.

"We weren't encouraged to study, everyone had jobs to do. I don't know how these were delegated. I recall rubbing dining room doors to remove all finger marks, herring and rubbing like mad, polishing the main oak staircase. Oh, I slipped from top to bottom of those stairs many a time, banging my bottom and head on each step! We helped with washing and mangling. Girls had a separate day for the laundry to the boys. We would have to turn the handles of big wooden mangles with heavy weights on them, one girl had the weight drop on her toe. My brother aged nine years was putting towels through and Freddie Reeves was turning the mangle handle as fast as possible but Gordon forgot to get his hand out of the way. He yelled and Freddie went into quick reverse but the damage was done, burst finger end. The sheets and clothes would be put onto big pulleys in the wall, and when dry, we'd fold them and thread them through the mangle again to save ironing. The girls would spend a lot of time in the sewing room, sewing linen buttons on our liberty bodices, darning socks, etc.

"We helped in the kitchen doing veg., slicing the long loaves on the slicer, fetching in the anthracite for the boilers, scrubbing the food slabs in the scullery. The dining room and corridor were beautiful herring bone style wooden floors, we polished those with a rectangle brush with a long handle, it had a reservoir for runny ronuk,(a liquid floor polish), and we'd go back and forward with it. Two of us would smash into each other and jump out of the way. Really you'd got to make fun as much as you could out of anything, as it was just taken as normal to be kept busy. We all used to dread getting the job of kneeling on the cold floor in the cloakroom to clean all the girls' boots. I recall being put in the bogey hole under the stairs where the brushes and mops were kept. It was pitch-black! I guess I'd been caught red-handed misusing the cleaning materials and sent to apologize to the mops.

"I didn't like my meat on a Sunday and would have to go without pudding and take my dinner into the kitchen. My brother would look sorrowfully at me as I took it in. I was told if I didn't eat it, I would have it for tea, as there were people starving and we should think ourselves lucky to have food. I suppose if they had been lenient with one, there could have been a lot of waste.

"I rang my brother Gordon last week in Portsmouth. We chatted for one and a half hours reminiscing. He said, 'Do you remember what we had for tea on weekdays?' and both together we said three half slices of bread and drippin' and a cup of cocoa. About twelve of us had the diphtheria germ and had to be in quarantine. We had to live in the recreation hall across the yard from the Home. Gordon reminded me of our supper treat of two small round ginger biscuits and a cup of café 'o' laite.

"We would put on pantomimes and concerts in the recreation hall, which was across the play area. I was short tongued till I was six, so had a lisp, and at the age of five, I was one of two daffodil bulbs that came through the ground too soon and was nipped by Jack Frost and died. My one line couldn't have had more S's in it! "And when the spirit of spring time comes she'll think that we are lost." I couldn't understand what folk were laughing at, according to my mum.

"Another time I was a tin soldier marching with several others to toy soldier parade, my brother was a golliwog. He had a tantrum on the night as he did not want his face blackened. Anyway, it was just smudged on. It must have been the Nutcracker, as all the toys came to life. Then yet another time we were slaves, dancing in a Persian market. We wore turbans on our heads, baggy trews and blouses in cerise, turquoise, purple, and orange fine voile. Those were fun filled times! (Author's note: I believe these concerts were fund-raising events.)

"At Christmas, I know we had parties. I think it was at the R.E.M.E. at Chilwell. We had some lovely gifts hand made by the soldiers there. At different parties, I had a roundabout of four horses going past a winning post, a wooden three-piece suit, and a sewing box. All the girls had their own initials painted at the top corner. We were very grateful for their kindness.

"Mrs. Starling of The Oaks, Broadgate, Beeston and Mrs. Simpson of Papplewick were governors, and we would go to their big houses sometimes to pick fruit. I recall matron standing at the end of our dining table with this basket of apples, rolling them down to us, laughing with us as we caught one.

"When we were practicing in the dining room, Matron had us singing around the piano, and she would pretend she couldn't read the music. She'd put her glasses on the end of her nose and point to the note and play it then another and play it, and so on to make us laugh. We respected her; she had a lovely smile, but not so nice if we were naughty as we had to take off a sandal to receive a smack on our hand with it, and if a stronger punishment was required, it was on your bottom, and always in front of everyone after mealtime. I suppose that was to prove a point of what you get if you don't conform. Several children used to run away, but they soon arrived back.

"We couldn't mix outside the home to play, but once I was given permission to go for tea to the house of Margaret Newbold whose parents owned the baker's shop at the bottom of Imperial Rd. I heard Uncle Mac on children's hour and she played the piano. I must add that we did go to see Mum once a month on a Saturday 10:00 a.m. till 6:00 p.m., and we'd spend a week with her at Christmas or summer at times.

"The following year, there were several meetings of parents and governors, etc., and I left in July 1946 and went home to live with Mum and brother. I hadn't known till this year why I went home at that time, but now understand there was different ownership of the building taking place."

"I never thought to query anything as we were always told to 'do as you are told and all will be fine.' That wouldn't be accepted by youngsters today."

I think that Brenda's final statement is most significant. In the conversations I have had with former residents of the Beeston Children's Homes, their acceptance of their situation and reluctance to question what happened to them and why has struck me quite forcibly. Nowadays, we are far more likely to challenge decisions which affect our lives. We question politicians, doctors, solicitors, and other professionals quite openly and hold them accountable for their actions. Back in the 1940/50s, things were very different.

I was thrilled to have learned so much about the Children's Homes from these former residents. I admired them greatly for their strength of character. Most were real "survivors" and had been able to rise above the harsh regime imposed upon them in the Homes. Many retained an admirable work ethic inculcated into them as "orphanage kids".

However, my journey of discovery was far from over. I still had so many unanswered questions. These included:

1. *Which agency or organization arranged my mother's adoption?*
2. *In view of her age, thirteen, why was she not fostered instead? In fact, if she was to be adopted at all, why wasn't she adopted when a baby, by a couple who wanted to make a lifelong commitment to her and bring her up as they would their own child?*
3. *What measures, if any, were taken to check that the Freemans were suitable adoptive parents?*
4. *Was her father's permission sought and obtained for the adoption? If not, why not?*

In time my stubborn persistence would ensure I got answers to some, if not all of my questions.

CHAPTER 8
Brick Walls

ANY DEALINGS I HAD WITH the Nottingham Councils' social work and adoption agencies in my attempts to find answers to my questions continued to result in frustration and disappointment. I believe that there were certain individuals who genuinely wanted to help me in my search, but for some reason, they were unable to progress the matter. Was it pressure of work, in-house protocols/procedures, red tape, lack of communication between agencies/ departments or intervention from higher up in the ranks? It was impossible for me to know. Maybe all these factors played a part. Because I so desperately needed to find answers to my questions, I found it difficult to accept that this whole matter was probably of little interest or consequence to others.

I was working full time, which left me precious little time to devote to my search. I was feeling physically, mentally, and above all emotionally exhausted. Most nights I would wake up in the early hours of the morning, everything churning over in my mind and wonder where I could turn next in my search for answers. I asked myself whether I should simply let the matter rest, but at the same time, I felt committed, as though I had started to drive down a one-way street and couldn't turn back. I simply had to press on although I had no idea exactly where I was headed or indeed how and when my "journey" would end. I tried to describe my feelings to one of the first social workers I came into contact with in a letter dated October 22, 2001:

> *"I am going through what I can only describe as a delayed grieving process for my Mum...I alternate between feelings of anger at the way other people have always decided which way her life should go, with disastrous consequences, and guilt because I along with most other people never really*

understood her, losing touch and therefore not being there for her when she finally decided to end it all back in 1985.

I also feel increasingly frustrated that it is such hard work to find out any information, as though it's nothing to do with me, and I don't have a right to know anything."

The Christmas holidays gave me almost two weeks' break in my busy routine. I had planned to decorate the study, but as I worked, there was a nagging feeling of frustration always lurking beneath the surface. I felt I had exhausted just about all the possibilities in my search. Worse still, I felt that no one truly understood how I was feeling, why getting my questions answered was so important to me.

I had read *Empty Cradles*, a book by the Nottingham social worker Margaret Humphreys who, in the 1980s, uncovered the scandal of the policy of the British government, assisted by most if not all the major children's charities, of sending disadvantaged children overseas, mainly to Australia, as "child migrants." This policy continued into the 1960s, and children were often sent without the knowledge or consent of their parents. Those who did know about it usually believed their children were going to be adopted by loving families and given a chance of a better life than they could give them. In most cases, these children were never adopted but continued to live in institutions and to be used as cheap labour. Some were told, erroneously, that their parents were dead and weren't given so much as a birth certificate as a link to their former life or their roots.

Many of them experienced sexual and/or physical abuse. In 1987, Margaret Humphreys established the Child Migrants Trust, a charity devoted to reuniting these children with their families in Britain.

As I read *Empty Cradles*, I could identify with the lack of communication on the part of the government, the local authorities, and charities. Their aim seemed to be not to redress the damage done to these children to help them find their true identities, but rather to protect themselves and their reputations, refusing to admit that, in hindsight, their policies had been flawed.

During the 1990s, extensive media coverage in the newspapers and on television brought the issue of child migration to the forefront of the public consciousness, and the various authorities and agencies involved could no longer realistically deny the part they had played.

In 1993, Margaret Humphrey's work on behalf of the child migrants was officially recognized by the Australian government when she was awarded the Order of Australia Medal by His Excellency the Governor-General Bill Hayden.

On Friday, August 31, 2001, the *Nottingham Evening Post* reported that, following an Australian inquiry into the scandal, remorse was expressed over the whole "sorry" episode. Later, the British government also officially apologized for the part they played in the policy of child migration and made funds available for the work of reuniting former child migrants with their families. I realized that my situation was different and that the Child Migrants Trust had to adhere to their remit to assist the former child migrants and their families, but I also felt sure that if anyone could understand my feelings and frustrations, Margaret Humphreys would. I therefore wrote a very long letter telling her the whole story and pouring out my frustration and disappointment at the way I felt I was being constantly sidelined.

I also wrote to Pam Hodgkins of NORCAP, a national agency committed to supporting adults affected by adoption, and requested her advice as to how I might proceed. Amongst other things, she suggested that it may be helpful for me to appeal to a local councillor to act as a go-between with the Notts County Council on my behalf.

In the meantime, once again information was to come from a totally unexpected and unconventional source. I had noticed that 26 Imperial Road, the house which was occupied by William Arthur and Lilian May Freeman when they adopted my mother in 1945, was up for sale. The house I lived in was only about two miles away, and when we bought it, there were all sorts of documents amongst the deeds, including a death certificate relating to the previous owner. I therefore dropped a note through the door of 26 Imperial Road asking if they had any information relating to previous occupants of the house, as I believed some relatives of mine had once lived there. Amazingly, I received the following reply dated December 17, 2001:

Dear Julie

I have been trying to trace my own ancestors and can certainly sympathize with the difficult task of tracking down relatives. Unfortunately, I do not have any paperwork relating to previous owners or residents. However, I did make enquiries with neighbours, who have told me that the previous owner was a letting company who let the property to a Mrs. Clarke. Apparently, Mrs. Clarke moved into the house in about 1947, probably after your relatives.

Mrs. Clarke is elderly but lives at (address given). My neighbours opposite keep in touch with her and she would have no objection to you contacting her.

I do hope Mrs. Clarke may be able to give you some useful information in your search. We have always found this a very happy house and often wondered who the past residents might have been…

I was becoming more and more aware of how interested people are in their ancestry. So many have tried to trace their "roots," at least to some extent, and possibly track down relatives. This is why they could empathize with me and wanted to help me in my search.

I lost very little time in paying Mrs. Clarke a visit. She now lived in a warden aided complex in Beeston, but prior to this had lived for many years at 26 Imperial Road with her husband and son. She told me that she knew Mr. and Mrs. Thursby at No. 36. Their daughter Lilian had moved into 26 Imperial Road around 1938 with her husband William Freeman. Mrs. Clarke and her husband heard through their friends that the Freemans intended to vacate the house in 1947, and they moved in after them. She didn't know why the Freemans were moving or where they went.

Mrs. Clarke was naturally curious about the reasons for my inquiries about Arthur and Lilian Freeman. She stated several times that they were childless and was possibly wondering, therefore, how I could be related to them. I told her that they had, in fact, adopted my mother, who up until that time had been brought up in the Children's Homes on Imperial Road. This jogged Mrs. Clarke's memory, and she said she did recall that they had taken in a child from the orphanage. This had been a surprise to the neighbours, who concluded that, as Lilian Freeman was a rather sickly woman, they probably wanted the girl to help around the house. However, she had not lived with them very long before suddenly disappearing off the scene.

I remarked to Mrs. Clarke how surprised I was that my mother had been legally adopted so late on in life and explained to her how my mother, if she had not been adopted, would have been entitled to a third of her sister Dorothy's estate. Due to her untimely death, she could no longer benefit from this legacy anyway, but under the intestacy laws, it would have passed to me. (My sister Jill would not have inherited because she herself was adopted.) A third of Dorothy's estate had amounted to £120,000. The decision to have my mother adopted was still, therefore, having repercussions on my life over sixty years later.

If my mother had been happy with the Freemans, if she had experienced a taste of what real family life was all about after spending almost her entire childhood in an institution, if they had been there at her wedding and loving grandparents to her children afterwards, the money would not have mattered. However, it seemed to me that nothing had been gained from her adoption and a great deal lost. The Freemans appear to have regarded my mother as little more than a skivvy. Had they realized the great responsibility, the depth of commitment which should be behind the decision to adopt a child, thereby severing any legal ties that child has with their birth family? Had anyone ever sat down and explained all this to them? I seriously doubted anyone had cared enough to do that, and my fears were later proved fully justified.

Mrs. Clarke listened with interest and expressed her sympathy, but she knew of other orphanage children who had been taken in by local families and been very happy. Alma Harvey, a girl from the orphanage who was six years older than my mother had lived with the Grays at 28 Imperial Road for many years and was regarded as one of the family, although Mrs. Clarke did not think she had ever been legally adopted by them. Mrs. Clarke believed, like many of her generation, that you simply had to accept the hand that life dealt out to you. There was no point looking back and wishing things had been different. What could that ever achieve?

I could see the logic in her argument, but I knew at the same time that something would drive me on. I needed to know, to understand, to make some sort of sense of it all. My mother was now dead. Any chance we may once have had to rekindle our relationship, at least in this life, was now lost. As a Jehovah's witness, my faith teaches me that we will one day be reunited with our dead loved ones, but when that time comes, I want to be able to say to my mother, "I know everything that happened, the whole story. No one told me, I found out for myself. I understand why you couldn't be a mother, but all that's in the past now, so let's make a fresh start."

Meeting someone who had actually known William Arthur and Lilian May Freeman, my pseudo "grandparents," aroused my curiosity in them even more. I wondered, could they possibly still be alive? If so, I would like to meet them. I was also very curious as to where they moved to in 1947 when they left the terraced house on Imperial Road.

Looking through the Beeston Parish Church Records at the Nottingham Archives, I came across an entry for the christening of Lilian May Thursby on June 27, 1906. She was born on May 24, 1906, and her parents were Albert Ewan and Louise Thursby. At the time of her christening, the family was living at 33 Church Street in Beeston. That meant that Lilian Freeman (nee Thursby) would now be ninety-five years old. It was possible she may still be alive, but unlikely, particularly as she had been a sickly woman most of her life.

My first search was for the record of William and Lilian's marriage. After some failed attempts, I eventually found the correct entry and ordered a copy of the marriage certificate. When it arrived, it showed that William A. Freeman had married Lilian May Thursby on July 30, 1932, at Beeston Parish Church. William was twenty-three and Lilian twenty six. I already knew from the parish records that Lilian was born in 1906. William was three or four years younger than her, so must have been born in 1909/10. That meant that he would be around ninety-one years old if he were still alive. It was a possibility I might still get to meet him.

It was now a question of painstakingly searching through the records of deaths for Freeman. I knew both William and Lilian had been alive in 1947. Mrs. Clarke had confirmed that she took over the tenancy of 26 Imperial Road from them in that year. They were at that time both quite young (William thirty-seven or thirty-eight and Lilian forty-one), so it seemed unlikely either of them would die in the 1940s. I therefore decided that my search would commence in 1950. As my time was limited, I commissioned the search company I had used previously to conduct a search of the death register on my behalf for the 1970s. When the results were returned, there was an entry for a Lilian May Freeman who had died in the Nottingham District, June quarter 1972 at sixty-six years of age. As I already knew that Lilian was borne on May 24, 1906, I was almost certain this was the correct person.

There was also an entry for a William A. Freeman who had died in 1979, which seemed to match the criteria, so there was a strong possibility that William too was dead. However, as I did not know his exact date of birth, I could not be absolutely sure. I therefore sent for the death certificate and waited for its arrival with some impatience. Even if this confirmed that I was too late to meet my adoptive grandfather, at least it may throw some light on where he had moved after leaving the house on Imperial Road, Beeston, in 1947.

CHAPTER 9
A Will but No Way

AUNT JOAN WAS DETERMINED THAT now she had found Audrey's children, Jill and I should get a third of Dorothy's inheritance. Her solicitors were in negotiation with John Green, Joan's brother and our uncle (although we had never met him). They were trying to draw up a deed whereby John and Joan would both voluntarily return a third of the £180,000 they had jointly shared, i.e. £60,000 each, to be shared equally between Jill and I as Audrey's surviving children. There was no legal obligation for either of them to do this, as a change in the adoption laws in 1949 determined that from January 1, 1950, an adopted child on intestacy should be treated as the natural child of their adoptive parents and not the child of anyone else. Hence at that time our mother lost any rights to inherit from Dorothy as her natural sister. However, Joan felt strongly that we, as Audrey's children, should inherit our mother's share, adoptions or no adoptions.

John Green had disagreed with Joan on this from the start, claiming that Mary, their younger sister, was no longer of the family due to her adoption, and they should therefore not worry about her. To some extent, I could understand his feelings, as he had a son and a daughter and they were no doubt his main priority. He had worked hard, despite his disadvantaged start in life, to get on and also to educate his children. His son had become a barrister and his daughter a doctor.

However, I felt that once John knew the full circumstances of his youngest sister's life, he would have a change of heart. Initially, he had not known how short-lived and unsuccessful her adoption had been; how at fifteen years of age she had absconded from the home of her adoptive parents and fended for herself; how she proved incapable of caring for her two daughters due to severe mental illness, resulting in her having a leucotomy and the second daughter being given up for adoption; how her marriage had faltered and ended in divorce; how she had tragically committed suicide at fifty-three years of age. Confronted with the full knowledge that Audrey had not been as successful as him in putting her past behind her, and how we had been affected as her daughters, I felt sure that he would soften and go along with Joan's wishes. However, this proved not to be the case.

For many months, letters went back and forth between Joan, her solicitors, and John. Before retirement, John spent the majority of his life in the legal profession, starting of course in 1942 when he was taken on by Mr. George Thornton Simpson, a trustee and chairperson of the committee of the Children's Homes, as a junior clerk in the legal firm of Acton, Marriott and Simpson. He therefore has a legalistic bent of mind, which requires that every *t* be crossed and every *i* dotted. He seems singularly unmoved by emotion of any sort. Once the deed was drawn up and forwarded to him for signature, he had further concerns relating to its wording. His chief concern seemed to be over such things as inheritance tax and how his estate would be affected should he "gift" any money to his nieces.

If Joan's incredible account of events related to Jill and I on our first visit in May 2001 are to be believed, she had inadvertently brought this unhappy situation upon herself. Joan told us that, shortly after arranging her own husband's funeral, she rushed down to London to be with Dorothy, who was in hospital dying of cancer. Dorothy did, in fact, die on March 28, 1999. Joan arrived later that same day, only to be told the sad news that she was too late by a matter of hours. To add to her grief, Joan was now faced with the task of single-handedly clearing out Dorothy's council flat at Carey Mansions, Westminster, and sorting out her estate. No doubt rather daunted by this, she readily accepted the help of a neighbour who had been friendly with Dorothy, Terence Carter.

Whilst they were sorting through Dorothy's papers one night, Joan numbing her grief by downing a couple of whiskies, Terence Carter drew her attention to an old will, which had been drawn up in 1982. The main beneficiary of this Will was Duncan Worsley, a longstanding boyfriend of Dorothy's who in fact lived with her for many years. The secondary beneficiary was Joan, and there were a couple of small bequests made to females who Joan assumed must be previous work colleagues or pupils of Dorothy's.

Joan knew that Duncan Worsley had died in 1985 but she assumed, incorrectly, that his share of Dorothy's estate would pass to any of his surviving family. Joan did not want this to happen because Dorothy had never received financial support from Duncan Worsley, in fact she believed he lived in the flat rent free. Having already determined to search for her long-lost brother and sister and wanting them to benefit from Dorothy's estate (although not knowing at this time, of course, how much it would amount to), Joan claims she rashly tore the will up. In actual fact, under the terms of that Will, as Duncan Worsley had died, Joan became the main beneficiary and would have inherited the entire estate, apart from the two minor bequests.

Thinking more clearly the following day, Joan realized how wrong it had been to destroy the will. However, she was too afraid to admit what she had done, fearing that she might even face a prison sentence. She therefore put the torn-up pieces of the document into a plastic bag and turned it over to the London solicitor she had asked to help her with the administration of the estate. She let the solicitor believe that she had found the will in that condition, and it was assumed that Dorothy had torn it up, thereby annulling the will. For months, Joan did not admit to what she had done, but let the settlement of the estate proceed on the basis of an intestacy, i.e. that Dorothy had not left a valid will. This meant that the estate should be shared equally between any siblings or, in the event of death of a sibling, their children.

Investigations were carried out to ascertain for sure that their younger sister, Mary, had indeed been legally adopted. John seemed fully convinced of this from the start, but unlike her brother, Joan had never really comprehended that Mary was "no longer of the family" and therefore had no right to inherit under Dorothy's estate. She wanted John to agree to jointly give their younger sister a third share of Dorothy's estate should she be traced. John was adamant he would not agree to this. Yet if Joan had not torn the will up, she would have inherited the entire estate and could have decided exactly what should happen to it and who should get what! Joan did not confess to her foolish deed until she received notification that the estate had been distributed equally between herself and John, in the amount of £180,000 each. Realizing that the money had been released, although no agreement had been reached between herself and John as to what would happen in the event Mary (or her daughters) could be traced in the future, Joan immediately got on the telephone to her London solicitor. In the fraught exchange which followed, Joan finally admitted to having destroyed the will (although she later claimed that in fact Terence Carter had torn it up at her request). The solicitor had immediately written to John Green, explaining to him that a mistake had been made and that he should return the £180,000 he had received immediately. Unsurprisingly, he did not do so.

John had endless questions about the way the estate had been administered by the solicitor and wanted full explanations for the way Joan had acted. He seemed to find it impossible to comprehend that a seventy-four-year-old widow, having recently lost her husband and sister in death within weeks of each other, having no children nor indeed any other known relations to support her at this difficult time, may not act completely rationally.

John wrote lengthy letters to Joan's solicitors maintaining that he was in absolutely no doubt that Dorothy had died intestate and that he was therefore fully entitled to the £180,000 he had received.

He requested that numerous amendments be made to the deed drawn up by Joan's solicitors and said he would only sign it if Joan would affirm that the will was already torn up when it was found, and that Dorothy therefore died intestate. This put Joan in a very difficult position legally. She had finally confessed to tearing the will up, so how could she now deny it?

Given John's intransigent attitude, I wanted to persuade Joan not to expend any more time and money in trying to reach an agreement with him through her solicitor. Her legal costs were mounting at an alarming rate, and I was feeling increasingly uncomfortable at the prospect of receiving any money from John Green anyway, as it was evident he totally begrudged it. Comments he made in correspondence with Joan's solicitor, to the effect that Jill and I meant absolutely nothing to him, betrayed the utter disdain he felt for his younger sister and her daughters. A remark to the effect that Jill and I had not even been close to our mother also hurt me deeply, since as children we obviously had no control over events which led to our estrangement from our mother and one another.

I decided to pen a letter to Joan, trying to word it in such a way that she would be persuaded to abandon her quest to "right the wrong." As far as I was concerned, we had now found our long-lost aunt and Joan her long-lost nieces, and we should make the best of the time we had to get to know each other and enjoy each other's company. If Joan wished to give Jill and me any of the money she had received which she felt should rightly have been our mother's, then she was free to do so.

When Joan made her regular telephone call on Wednesday evening, she said that she had read the letter over and over again, and that it "said it all." She had been greatly moved by it, but not, sadly, in the direction I had hoped. She was as determined as ever to continue to fight John on this matter. She felt that he had scorned all three of his sisters by the way he had acted. Nevertheless, Joan was content for John to have his share of Dorothy's inheritance, provided he returned a third for the children of his youngest sister. If he were not prepared to do this, it was Joan's intention to fully contest the matter in court on the basis that the will had been wrongly administered.

Joan asserted that she would merely fester inwardly if she dropped the matter now. I so wished she would, could let go.

Was the money of any importance to me at all? I would be lying if I said it wasn't. Stephen and I have always been in the lower-income bracket. Now he was struggling, due to ill health, to keep working full time, and we had a hefty mortgage to pay each month. Our daughter had recently married, and I was saddened that she and her husband had to pay for the majority of their wedding because we had very little saved, and it has never been our policy to go into debt.

However, to me there is far more significance attached to wills and inheritances than these immediate monetary concerns. A person's will makes a final statement. For instance, when my great-grandmother died, she left two children, my grandmother Lucy, and her older sister Phyllis. Phyllis moved away to live in London and indeed we hardly ever saw her. In contrast, my grandmother Lucy continued to live nearby and, despite having eight children, including my father, she was always expected to help her mother, who never showed her any appreciation whatsoever. Finally, she nursed her mother through a very difficult illness until she died. When her mother's will was read, she had left money to both daughters, but a significant amount more to Phyllis. I can remember the sadness in my grandmother's voice when she said, "I always thought Phyllis was her favourite, and now I know I was right."

When my grandmother Lucy died in 1977, although I had been brought up by her after my parent's divorce, the little money she left was split between her eight children. It only amounted to a few hundred pounds each, and she expressed in her will that she would like them to maybe give me a token amount, which indeed some of them did. However, it made me realize that, at the end of the day, I didn't really belong in this family. Anything I received was a "gift," not a right.

When my father died in 1980 at only forty-nine years of age from cancer, my stepmother Eileen was left alone to cope with three young children, my half-brother and two half-sisters. Naturally, they were my dad's chief concern, as I was already married, so everything was left to my stepmother. How much a small keepsake, perhaps his signet ring, would have meant to me, as a token of his recognition of me as his eldest daughter, although I had not lived with him since I was five years of age.

When my stepmother herself died about ten years later, also of cancer, her children did not contact me with the news until after her funeral, and there was certainly no mention of me being entitled to any share, along with them, in the property she left.

When Jill's adoptive mother died, she and her adopted sister Rosemary shared the proceeds of the estate. I remember remarking to Jill that Stephen would inherit along with his brother and sister when his parents died, but that I had never been the beneficiary in a will, nor expected to be. I tried to explain to her that it wasn't so much the money which mattered as knowing that you indisputably belonged to a family; that it went without question that you would receive an inheritance, large or small, simply by virtue of the fact that you were a member of that family. At the end of the day, it is the ultimate test of whether you truly belong to anyone, whether you "fit in" anywhere. It was constantly being reaffirmed in my mind that I didn't, and that hurt.

Approaching Christmas 2001, Joan's solicitor appeared to be getting near to a settlement with John Green over the signing of the deed. Two copies had been drawn up and sent to Joan and John for signature. I had reservations because I knew that John had requested certain amendments to the deed and didn't fully know what these were or understand how they might affect Aunt Joan. I spoke to Joan on the telephone about my concerns and encouraged her to question the nature of the amendments which had been made before signing and returning the deed, but there was no reasoning with her. Joan had no qualms about signing and returning the deed, despite the reservations I had expressed to her. She further had money transferred from her bank account to her solicitor so that they would be able to match John's £60,000 with her £60,000 and jointly forward these monies on to Jill and me as Mary's daughters. That, as far as Joan was concerned, would be the end of the matter.

Then, one evening I received an astonishing telephone call from Joan. She said that she had done something which I might think very foolish, but it was done now and couldn't be undone. She had sent John a Christmas card, but not put who it was from. Inside the Christmas card, she had put what was in reality rose fertilizer, but which could easily be mistaken for anthrax powder. I was absolutely speechless!

On September 11, 2001, just three months prior to this, Al-Qaeda terrorists had flown two planes into the Twin Towers in New York, and President George Bush had launched his "war on terror." The Western World was on full alert for further terrorist atrocities, and letters sent to high profile individuals had been intercepted in the mail because they contained anthrax. At any time, this was a very odd way for a senior citizen in her seventies to act. Under the circumstances, it was the very worst of times. For the next couple of weeks, Stephen and I wondered if Joan, or even we, might be paid a visit by the terrorist squad! Up until this time, I had not fully comprehended what a truly eccentric individual Joan was!

It came as no great surprise to me that John Green did not sign and return the deed as requested. Had Joan's actions influenced his decision and made him decide not to co-operate? Possibly, but having spent a lifetime in the legal profession, John was incapable of agreeing to such a straightforward compromise. As I stated earlier, he wanted every *t* crossed, every *i* dotted. He was adamant that "this appalling state of affairs is entirely of Joan's own making," which was, strictly speaking, true. John had, however, benefited very handsomely from Joan's foolhardiness in destroying the will.

By February 2002, John had still not agreed to sign the deed. He became very critical of the way Dorothy's estate had been administered by Joan's solicitors. Why hadn't they done this? Why hadn't they queried that? I have to say that I am not entirely happy with the way they handled the matter either, especially as I believe they made the final distribution of the estate without Joan's express consent as administratrix, but I felt no justification in complaining because, when all was said and done, Joan had apparently not been completely honest with them from the beginning.

She had allowed them to believe that Dorothy's will was already torn up when it was found and only confessed to having been a party to its destruction after the proceeds of the estate were distributed, twelve months after Dorothy's death.

Having now accepted Joan's later version of events, that she had ripped up the will, as the truth, it would be very difficult for her solicitors to agree to John Green's terms, i.e. that "the deed would have to be drawn up strictly on the basis that Dorothy died intestate and that I am an equal beneficiary," as they would then, of course, be a party to a lie.

Joan's "trump card" in the event of negotiations with John breaking down, was to refer the matter to the Chancery Court for them to make a declaration as to the validity of the will and the distribution of the estate under it. It was now looking increasingly likely that this would be the only course of legal redress available to her—but more on this later.

CHAPTER 10
A Breakthrough

AROUND MARCH 2002, EDITION ONE of *Nottinghamshire County News* was pushed through our door, a new newspaper for Nottinghamshire, produced by Notts County Council "to keep everyone better informed about the work of the Council and what's going on across the county."

The lead story on the front page of this local authority publication began:

"Nottinghamshire County Council is backing an international conference in New Orleans this autumn on the highly emotive subject of child migration..."

The article pointed out that the Notts County Council "was for a long time the main source of financial backing for West Bridgford based charity The Child Migrant's Trust which provides counselling and a tracing service to help re-unite families of former child migrants."

Councillor Mick Warner, the leader of Nottinghamshire County Council, was quoted as saying:

"A large group of our citizens were torn from their families at an early age and sent half a world away. We have a responsibility to these people to do what we can now to put this right...This first international congress of the Child Migrants Trust will be a small step along the road to reparation, and I am delighted that Nottinghamshire County Council is once again leading the way with a £20,000 loan to the trust to help it organize the conference."

About three months previously, Pam Hodgkins of Norcap had advised me to involve a county councilor in my fight to be allowed to access my mother's adoption records. If Mick Warner was as genuinely concerned as this article suggested about these issues, I decided he may be the best one to contact. I drafted a letter which began:

> Dear Councillor Warner
>
> I am writing to you following receipt of the first edition of Nottinghamshire County News and after reading the front page feature on the Council's intention to back an international conference on the highly emotive subject of child migration.
>
> I was greatly encouraged to see evidence that Notts County Council is not only fully aware of but very sympathetic towards the plight of youngsters who, through no fault of their own, were put into the care of agencies and organizations who did not always act in the children's best interests.
>
> I am sure that, through its close association with the Child Migrants Trust, the Council also fully appreciates how far reaching the consequences of past decisions made on behalf of those children have been to them and their families, and how important it is that past mistakes are openly admitted and every assistance given to either reunite those children with their relatives or, if it is too late for that, to at least be as frank and open as possible about the reasons these decisions were made, however embarrassing to the agencies concerned.
>
> I wonder if you are aware that it was not only children who were shipped abroad who experienced mistreatment and abuse? ...

I went on to explain to Councillor Warner all I knew regarding my mother's background, her upbringing in the Beeston Children's Homes, her adoption, failed marriage to my father, and how this had resulted in my sister Jill and me being brought up separately, and finally our mother's suicide. I continued:-

> So why am I writing to you? Because, although I have discovered a great deal through my own research, I still have some key questions and I will not be able to reach closure on this and move on until I have them answered...
>
> I would like a county councillor to exercise their influence for me to gain access to the archived records of the agency which

arranged my mother's adoption...This file may contain the answers to some of my questions...I already know the identity of Mary's natural parents and her adoptive parents and Mary herself is dead, so the argument that this information cannot be revealed in order to protect the adopted child is irrelevant. Mary is the only one who hasn't been protected in all this...I trust that you will give serious consideration as to how I can be assisted to find truthful answers to my questions.

Two weeks later, I received a telephone call from Councillor Warner in which he expressed regret over the sad circumstances of my mother's life and said that he had urged Notts Social Services to co-operate with me in finding answers to my questions. He also wrote to me saying that the contents of my letter had been noted with "interest and concern" and that the director of Social Services "is presently looking into the issues raised in your letter and will write back to you as soon as possible."

Despite Councillor Warner's interceding on my behalf, it was November 2002 before I was finally allowed to see my mother's adoption records. This was seven months after I wrote to Councillor Warner and fifteen months after I first requested Notts County Council to be allowed to do so. The waiting seemed interminable, but I busied myself with my visits to the archives, gradually piecing together more information.

On one lunchtime visit to the archives, I looked in the card index system under orphanages and saw an entry pertaining to the Children's Homes at Beeston. Searching out the larger, more detailed index, it directed me to a Notts County Council Education Committee file referenced CATC 10/110/45, stating that it related to the handover of the Homes to the Notts County Council. My interest was immediately aroused. However, I noted that, in keeping with other information about the Homes contained at the Archives, this file was also marked "Restricted."

I approached the archivist at the desk and inquired whether "Restricted" applied to the entire file or just a section of it. He perused the index for a moment and then asked me what my interest in the file was. I explained that my mother, two aunts, and an uncle had been residents there as children and I was doing research into the history of the Homes. The archivist remarked that he was surprised that the file was in fact restricted as, unlike the committee meeting minutes relating to the Homes, this file dealt with the building and was unlikely to make specific reference to the children in residence. He therefore decided to de-restrict the file and wrote his reasons for doing so in the index.

Ten minutes later, I went into the area reserved for researchers examining documents which are not on general display, was handed the file I had specifically requested, and settled down to browse through it. On the front page was the following heading:-

Town Clerk's Office, Education Committee
Children's Home, Beeston.
Transfer to Education Committee
17 March 1947–8 June 1948

I suppose the contents of that file would have made very dry reading indeed to anyone who had no prior interest or knowledge about the Homes. However, to me it made compulsive reading. No masterfully written thriller or whodunit could have entranced me more. I became so engrossed that returning to work before I had mentally assimilated all its contents was out of the question. I telephoned to say that I would not be coming back that afternoon and continued reading, hardly believing the events which were unfolding before me. I returned within the next few days, this time to make notes on the file. The following is a brief summary of its contents:-

Mr. George Thornton Simpson approached the Nottingham Corporation in early 1947 offering to make the most generous gesture of "gifting" the Homes to them. He explained that they had been experiencing staffing problems and the health of both the long-serving matron, Mrs. Freeman, and deputy matron, Mrs. Haslam, was beginning to suffer due to the demands of running the Homes with so few staff. He stated that it was also becoming increasingly difficult to raise the necessary funds to continue running the Homes as a charitable concern. Nottingham Corporation were likewise keen to transfer "maladjusted children" from the premises they were already using at Farnsfield, which were deemed to be too small and hence unsuitable, and the wheels were set in motion to transfer ownership.

In a letter from Mr. Thornton Simpson to Mr. Stephenson of the Nottingham Education Committee dated April 2, 1947, Mr. Thornton Simpson stressed that he and Mr. Starling, the two principal trustees of the Beeston Children's Homes, wished to transfer ownership of the Homes on or before July 1, 1947, because they simply could not envision being able to continue running them after that time.

By this time, the number of children in residence at the Homes had been whittled down to only fourteen. The Homes were capable of housing over forty children and had, in the past, been fully occupied. Of the remaining fourteen, six were to return to their families, one was working at the Homes, and seven were to be transferred to other Nottingham Corporation children's homes. Following that, it was the intention of the Education Committee to transfer to the Homes the staff and children from the Child Guidance Hostel at Farnsfield.

An agreement to hand over the Homes was made on June 10, 1947, and a "handing over ceremony" was planned for July 1, to be attended by Mr. Richards, the town clerk. The lord mayor would also be present to accept the trustees' generous gift, and Alderman Hall would formerly express the thanks of the Notts Education Committee. The conveyance of the premises was completed on July 24, 1947. The property was renamed Silverwood Hall and was run as a hostel for maladjusted boys by the Nottingham City Council until the late 1950s/early 1960s.

However, two complications arose. Firstly, the Children's Homes had been established in the early 1880s by Catherine Bayley as a privately run charitable institution subject to the terms of a trust deed. So, despite Mr. Simpson's generous offer to "gift" them to the Nottingham Corporation, the Homes were not strictly his to give away!

Secondly, Mrs. Mary Elizabeth Littlewood, nee Bradshaw, a wealthy Nottingham widow resident at Cavendish Crescent North, The Park, Nottingham, died on June 20, 1947, aged ninety-three years, just ten days after the agreement to hand over the Homes was drawn up and before the transfer of the Homes to the Nottingham Corporation was completed. In her last will, which was signed and witnessed on May 23, 1946, and revoked any former wills, she bequeathed £20,000 to the Children's Homes at Beeston, a huge amount in 1947, the generosity of which can only properly be appreciated when translated into today's values. For example, the property itself was valued at £4,000 in 1947. Mrs. Littlewood's bequest therefore amounted to five times the value of the property itself.

There were four alternatives as to what should now happen to the money.

1) It should be given to the former trustees of the children's homes.
2) It should be given to the Nottingham City Council.
3) The bequest should fail.
4) The cy-pres doctrine should be applied.

Cy-pres doctrine—The legal doctrine that allows a court freedom in interpreting the terms of a will or gift if carrying out the terms literally would be impracticable or illegal. At the same time, the general intent of the testator or donor is supposed to be observed as closely as possible.

Mr. H. B. E. Horrell, legal advisor for the Ministry of Education, in a letter dated October 23, 1947, requesting his advice, stated:

"I can see no reason why the Executors should not pay the money to the former Trustees of the Homes and, if they do this, they will have fulfilled their duty and it will then be for the Trustees of the Homes to dispose of the money."

However, Messrs. Tutin and Co., executors of Mrs. Littlewood's will, sought counsel's opinion of Mr. J. V. Nesbitt, Lincoln's Inn, on December 15, 1947. He concluded:-

"The trustees of this charity had no right or power at all to enter into this agreement of June 10, 1947...If it were practically impossible to carry on this charity, then it was the duty of the committee to apply either to the Charity Commissioners or to the Court and ask them to make a scheme for the charity cy-pres." He further advised, *"The executors should write to the Treasury Solicitor, putting all the facts before him..."*

Once appraised of the situation, the treasury solicitor, in a letter dated February 3, 1948, questioned by what authority the Notts

Corporation had acted, as "it would appear that the application of the property of the charity contemplated by the agreement could only have been effected by a scheme of the Minister of Education, of the Charity Commissioners or of the Court."

H. O. Danckwerts, counsel for the Attorney General, in an opinion dated March 11, 1948, strongly condemned the steps which the Notts Corporation and the trustees of the Homes had taken stating, "In my opinion, the agreement and disposition of the assets of the Nottingham Children's Homes was wholly unlawful." Counsel's opinion was sought of Humphrey H. King, 5 New Square, Lincoln's Inn on behalf of the town clerk. He said he had to agree with the opinion expressed by Danckwerts and at a meeting on May 5, 1948, he suggested that the trustees make an application to the court for a scheme authorizing the use of the Homes as a Child Guidance Hostel, otherwise if unsuccessful the property would revert to the trustees, who would have to administer it according to the trusts.

On May 12, 1948, the town clerk wrote to Mr. George Thornton Simpson, as trustee of the Homes, expressing his hope that they would not have to hand the "gift" back. He continued…

"The matter is still complicated by the £20,000 (Mrs. Littlewood's bequest), and I am afraid that as long as the disposal of that sum is outstanding, our actions will be subject to scrutiny by the attorney general who will probably be only too ready to challenge any attempt by the Minister of Education or by us to deal with the matter otherwise than in accordance with the opinion of the Counsel for the Attorney General."

The file ends very inconclusively with a note of a telephone conversation between the Notts Corporation and Mr. Thornton Simpson dated June 8, 1948. It reads:

"Mr. Thornton Simpson rang up to say that he has just heard from his London agents (Messrs. Peacock and Goddard) that they have been asked by the treasury solicitor to postpone any proceedings in respect of the Children's Home. The treasury solicitor is apparently in touch with the Minister of Education and the Charity Commissioners and there would seem to be a hope that the matter will be settled without an application to the court…"

I sat motionless for a long time afterwards, feeling thrilled to have unearthed this information relating to the institution which had played such a large part in the lives of my family, but also fearful that these events may be the key to explaining why my mother was adopted so unsuccessfully at thirteen years of age and why arrangements had to be made for so many other children to vacate the Homes, a number of whom were also adopted.

Surely anyone reading this file would conclude, as I did, that this was obviously not the full story. Two unanswered questions immediately spring to mind:

1. After such a legal deadlock had developed and against the opinion of three separate barristers, how was a way found to settle this matter without application to the court?
2. What actually happened to the money left in Mrs. Littlewood's will to an institution which, in effect, no longer existed?

On a more personal note, the following two questions concerned me:

1. Were the adoptions, which took place around this time, on the basis that the Homes were "closing down," in the best interests of the children concerned (including my mother), or simply an attempt to clear the Homes of as many children as possible so that the Notts Corporation could take it over quickly and easily without having to relocate too many children?
2. Were Mr. Simpson's motives in "gifting" the Children's Homes to the Notts Corporation totally philanthropic, or did he have prior knowledge of the bequest that Mrs. Littlewood had made in her will and hope to benefit personally?

On my second visit to take notes on the file, I spoke to one of the archivists and told him that this file ended very inconclusively, and there must surely be further files on the subject. I pointed out to him that, in the indexes, it stated that there was information up until 1958. However, the archivist assured me that there were no further files, saying that the year 1958 in the index was no doubt a typing error. He subsequently amended it to read 1948.

I was very troubled by what I had read in the file. Did its contents mean something or nothing? Was George Thornton

Simpson a saint or a sinner? Without further information on how the matter was resolved, it was impossible to know.

The *Nottingham Evening Post* of September 27, 1949, reports that the attorney general later directed the Nottingham City Council to pay the former trustees of the Homes £5,050 for the building, including fixtures and fittings, even though it had originally been handed over as a "gift." However, no information regarding what happened to Mrs. Littlewood's £20,000 bequest has yet been unearthed.

Interestingly, the *Nottingham Evening Post* of October 8, 1947, carried the headline "Big Nottingham Bequests—Doctor's Widow Leaves £598,443." It goes on to report that the Salvation Army Eventide Home at Radcliffe-on-Trent and the Family Welfare Committee of the Nottingham Council of Social Service were also left £20,000 each in Mrs. Littlewood's will.

CHAPTER 11
Mother Was a Stranger

I HAD IMAGINED, AFTER COUNCILLOR Mick Warner had given me his backing in March 2002, that I would soon be able to locate and access my mother's adoption file, or at least receive confirmation as to whether it still existed. However, over four months went by before I received a letter from Notts County Council Social Services, dated July 29, 2002.

A social worker, Ms. P, had apparently spoken to the General Register Office in Southport, who had informed her that it is unlawful for information to be shared with anyone who is not the adopted person and that any challenges to this had to go to the high court.

She had then written to the designated care judge at the County Court, asking for his advice as to whether there was any way I could access my mother's adoption records.

The designated care judge had confirmed that it was unlawful to disclose the records, "if they still exist," to anyone other than the adopted person but was giving the matter further consideration.

"If they still exist…If they still exist." I had heard this phrase so many times. It was now almost eighteen months since I had started to approach the council and various agencies with a request to find, and access, my mother's adoption file. Yet I could still not be sure whether it even existed. How could I break this repetitive cycle and make some headway in finding the answers I so badly needed to know?

I had written an article which I hoped to get published in the Nottingham Evening Post. The whole story had become so complex that it was difficult to sum it up in a short article, but I had two objectives in mind, and I tried to write down only the information which would help me to achieve these. The first objective was to encourage other people with firsthand knowledge of the Children's

Homes to come forward. Just a couple of sentences in the Questions from Readers section of the Nottingham Evening Post had previously put me in contact with the Metcalf family, whose reminiscences about life in the Homes had been so helpful. I was sure a larger article would motivate many more former residents to contact me. Secondly, I wanted to put pressure on the "powers that be," if possible, to make a decision in favour of allowing me to see my mother's adoption file.

After a great deal of effort, I managed to condense the relevant parts of the story into just 1,342 words. It was to be published in "Bygones," a regular Monday night feature in the Nottingham Evening Post. The article was accompanied by the two photos of the Children's Homes, which Violet Metcalf had supplied me with, and a photo of Aunt Joan, Jill, and myself.

The headline read "MOTHER WAS A STRANGER" and the article began:

> JULIE Leek's search for her roots led her to a long forgotten children's home and the truth about the mother she hardly knew. Now she asks Bygones to help piece together more details about the story...
>
> To Julie Leek, her mother was a stranger. It is only in recent months, as she searches into her mother's background, that she is uncovering the tragic details of her life—and her real name...

The article, along with photographs, made quite an impressive two-page spread, but would it achieve its twofold objective? My contact details were cited at the end of the article in the hopes that people would get in touch.

Following publication of the article, I received several telephone calls from people with whom it had struck a chord.

Mrs. Burrows, still a resident of Beeston, rang me to say that she remembered Mary Green well. She had been a tiny, fragile looking little girl, and knowing that she was a resident at the Children's Homes, Mrs. Burrows and a friend had treated her kindly at school, often bringing little treats and giving them to her in the playground.

"We've often wondered whatever happened to Mary Green," she said sadly, "and now we know."

Muriel Powell, nee Goodband, rang to say that four of her family had spent a few months in the Children's Homes when their mother was seriously ill with meningitis. They lived nearby and longed for the day when they could return home. Her brother, Alec Goodband, had been sweet on Mary Green and had sneaked into the girls' half of the Homes one night to give her a good night kiss. He was found and given a slippering. Muriel was born in 1931, the same year as Mary, and remembered her well.

Muriel's happiest memory of her time at the Homes was when there was a spare ticket for the Christmas pantomime, and she was chosen to go. Those left behind were given an especially nice tea as compensation. Her worst memory was of feeling sick at the dinner table one evening because she did not like the pearl barley, which was in the stew. She left the dining room and headed for the toilets to be sick, but the matron, Mrs. Freeman, followed her in a rage and was pushing the food back in with a spoon as quickly as Muriel vomited it out. In the one telephone conversation I had with Olwen Reddish, Mrs. Freeman's daughter, she mentioned that her mother had become ill prior to the Children's Homes being handed over to the Nottingham City Council, and I thought that her behavior on this occasion was probably evidence of this, as it could scarcely be described as balanced or normal. Perhaps the stress of running the Homes was all becoming too much for her.

Robert "Bobby" Hill, born in 1927 and then living in Chorley, Lancashire, rang to say that he was the youngest of seven children and had been a resident in the Beeston Children's Homes between 1929 and 1939 before finally being reunited with his family. He had recently made a nostalgic trip back to Beeston and had been reminiscing about the Children's Homes in the pub one night. Someone had kindly sent the article to him in the post, knowing that he would find it of interest.

Bobby remembered John Green as a pal. He also remembered Ms. Lovelock, Mrs. Hallam and Mrs. Freeman, remarking, "They were all martinets (i.e. strict disciplinarians). They would all be up in court today."

Later, I had the pleasure of meeting Bobby when he visited relatives in Beeston. We talked about his memories of the Beeston Children's Homes, and he was able to independently recall similar experiences to other former residents. For example, he had vivid memories of being force-fed fatty meat he had left from a previous mealtime and of a boy who had wet the bed being draped with the soiled sheet and humiliated in front of the others. We reflected on the fact that the Homes seem to hold a kind of fascination for the children who lived there, and when visiting the area, they often feel drawn to return to the place where the building once stood despite unhappy memories.

Following our meeting, Bobby wrote: "I'm sure I speak for all the orphanage kids when I say thank you Julie and God bless you for the time and trouble you have taken with your research into our childhood. It's a story that should be told and part of Beeston's social history that should be remembered."

Finally, I received a letter from my dad's eldest sister, my aunt Kath. My dad had six sisters, and Kath had always been my favourite aunt. I had stayed at her home in Clifton on a number of occasions when a youngster. I type it just as she wrote:

> *Dear Julie*
>
> *After reading your article in the Evening Post, I thought I would write to you in reply to it. The first encounter that I had with your Mother, was she was living at Portland House when she met your father. When they married I remember meeting Joan and Dorothy at 35 Commercial Street, although I didn't know anything about her very young life, but she herself told me that she was adopted by the Freemans and that her real name was Mary Green. As time went by she seemed very unhappy, I don't think she could settle to being married and when she was pregnant with you she did tell me that she had nothing to live for, I don't know why but she used to confide in me quite a lot. After you were born she had a nervous breakdown, and your father was very worried because she became very suicidal, like when he came home from work he would find her trying to gas herself, and that happened on one or two occasions, so eventually she had to*

go into Mapperley Hospital where she had a brain operation, that was why your father had to ask his mother & father to take care of you, as he had to work and when Jill was born, he was advised to have her adopted on the grounds of your mother's illness, and no one in the family apart from your Dad ever saw Jill as she was taken away from them soon after she was born, of course your Dad was very upset, but under the circumstances what could he have done, but Julie I know that you were brought up with your Grandma & Grandad and they thought the world of you, and so did we all. I hope you will forgive me for telling you this, but maybe all that will put some of the events of her life into perspective…

P.S. Julie your Dad thought the world of Audrey, but he could not cope with the way things were with her, he did try his very best but it all resulted in the breakdown of the marriage, maybe he didn't realize what was behind all her young life, that may have caused it all, it is only what I read in your article that made me realize.

-Love Auntie Kath

Dear Aunt Kath. She was such a kind and loving person, especially to children. Of course, I now knew everything she had written in her letter, but if she had talked to me about it when a child, she could have told me things I didn't know, such as my mother's real name. I suppose adults think they are being kind to children if they shield them from unpleasant realities, but children need to know the truth as much as anyone else.

Aunt Kath had said in her letter that my article had made her stop and think that probably my mother's childhood had been the cause of her depression and inability to cope with married life, and I hoped that others in the family, if they read the article, might be moved to think more kindly of her too. Sadly, I can honestly say that in all the time I was growing up, I never heard anyone in the family say a kind word about my mother, although my grandmother always made it a policy never to speak ill of anyone either. I was pleased that all these people had contacted me, especially as Mrs. Burrows and Muriel Powell both remembered my mother personally. However, I had especially hoped that other children who had been adopted, like my mother, would come forward. The Beeston Children's Homes had become an Adoption Society in 1943, and I knew the names of at least three other children who had been adopted. I wondered if their adoptions had been any more successful than that arranged for my mother. Sadly, none of them came forward.

What about my second objective, to hopefully exert some pressure on the authorities to allow me to see my mother's adoption file?

As soon as I knew the date when my article would be published in the *Nottingham Evening Post*, I wrote a reply to the letter I had received from Nottinghamshire Social Services on July 29, and also sent a copy to various professionals that I had been in contact with since the start of my search, most of whom were mentioned in the body of my letter. I hoped the publication of the newspaper article and my letter arriving on their desks the same day might cause a bit of a stir. The salient points are as follows:

> Dear Ms. P...
>
> *GLADYS MARY GREEN/ LILIAN AUDREY FREEMAN ADOPTION BY WILLIAM ARTHUR & LILIAN MAY FREEMAN IN 1945*
>
> *Thank you for your letter dated 29 July 2002 updating me on the position in relation to accessing my mother's adoption papers. I was somewhat surprised to hear that it is actually unlawful for me as the closest surviving relative of my deceased mother to be given information from her adoption file.*
>
> *During the course of the past year, I have received letters from the following social work professionals:*
>
> **Four names and positions listed but omitted due to Data Protection.*
>
> > *All of these have separately encouraged me to contact various adoption agencies, such as the Salvation Army, Catholic Children's Society, Barnardos, and others for records checks. Surely, as they belong to a caring*

profession and were trying to help me, they would not have encouraged me to make these enquiries if it was a foregone conclusion that, even if I did track down my mother's adoption file, I would not be allowed to see it! For the past year, I have been under the assumption that the problem was locating the file rather than not being allowed to see it when and if it was found...

The possibility that my mother's adoption records may have been destroyed has been mentioned to me on several occasions, and in your latest letter you again bring this into question, saying, "IF they still exist," so that even now I am left wondering if this is a futile quest. Surely the logical, not to mention the compassionate course, would be to determine beforehand whether or not her adoption records do still exist. If they do not, then there is no point keeping me in anxious suspense whilst a judge gives consideration as to whether I should be allowed to see them.

Of course, I fully appreciate that there is a need for confidentiality in these matters to protect the adopted child. However, in the case of my mother, her mother died in 1933 when she was under two years of age, her father died in the 1960s, her adoptive parents, with whom she lived for under 3 years, both died in the 1970s—so who is there left to protect?

Perhaps I should be grateful that at least she was not shipped abroad as a child migrant, but quite frankly it is impossible to imagine that her life could have turned out any more tragically if she had been. At least most of the child migrants were never adopted, and so they are still legally bound to their families if and when they do find them. For example, Councillor Warner told me of the very sad case of a former child migrant who came over from Australia to be reunited with her family, but her mother died a week before she arrived.

This is conjecture, but supposing the mother, now a widow, had two other children who she was able to keep? Unwisely, she had not made a Will, but she naturally assumed that her surviving children would inherit her estate. Would the child who had been shipped abroad as a child migrant but never adopted have a claim to a third of the estate? Legally, I believe she would, and morally, if the mother had known what had become of her, she would probably have wanted her to inherit along with her other children!

In my mother's case, she was one of four siblings who grew up together in the Beeston Children's Home, but the only one to be adopted. In 1999 her sister Dorothy died. She had never married or had children but left a considerable amount of money. Her sister Joan, who had always remained in contact with Dorothy, initiated a search for her other brother and sister (my mother) who she had long ago lost contact with. Her brother was found very easily, but she could not trace my mother. Joan wanted her brother and sister to also benefit from Dorothy's estate. Under the intestacy laws, she believed it would automatically be split three ways between herself, her brother, and sister (my mother). As it turned out, my mother was no longer alive anyway, but even before this was known the brother, who was quite knowledgeable about the law because he worked for many years in the legal profession, pointed out to Joan that as their youngest sister had been adopted (albeit at 13 years of age and very unsuccessfully), she was "no longer of the family" and therefore not entitled to inherit along with them. He advised Joan not to spend any more time and money on trying to trace her because he considered it "pointless."

Legally he was correct, and Dorothy's estate was split between the two of them. However, her brother's attitude toward my mother and his refusal to cooperate with Joan in agreeing to share some of their inheritance if and when she was traced caused such a rift between him and Joan that tragically, after being put back in contact with each other again after almost 60 years, they now no longer speak to each other.

So, I hope this illustrates what a huge decision it is to have someone adopted out of their own family, and what long term implications it can have. There should surely be only one valid reason for any adoption— that it is in the child's best interests. (*End of letter*)

In all, copies of this letter were sent to eight other persons/organizations who had helped or advised me over the last year. I felt I had nothing to lose by bringing the whole affair into the open and possibly a lot to gain. I was playing my trump card, and as I had no other cards up my sleeve, I certainly hoped to sway opinion in my favour.

Although the law at present stipulates that the adopted person alone should be granted access to their adoption records, I knew that my mother would never have requested such permission on her own account, as she belonged to a generation which believed it had no right to question people in authority and had absolutely no sense of her own identity or self-worth because of being institutionalized most of her life. If she had still been alive and we had been reunited, she may have had the courage to request access to her records at my suggestion and with my support. However, she had taken her own life seventeen years earlier, and as her closest surviving relative, I strongly believed that I had a right to see my mother's adoption file, particularly as it may help me to make sense of everything that had happened.

Did the *Evening Post* article and my letter achieve the desired result? I had to wait a further five weeks to find out.

CHAPTER 12
The Freemans

MY SISTER JILL AND I had both made several trips to visit Joan after our initial reunion in May 2001, and we were always trying to persuade her to visit us in Nottingham. However, she had maintained she would not come whilst affairs with her brother John were still not settled. The matter had dragged on and on for so long, however, that she finally consented to paying us a visit. Jill visited her in Wales in August 2002 and brought her back by car. She stayed part of the time with Jill and part of the time with me.

We visited the Workhouse Museum at Southwell where Joan's mother (maternal grandmother to me and Jill), had died in the infirmary from tuberculosis in 1933. Joan vaguely remembered being driven there in a big black car with her younger siblings Dorothy and John to see her shortly before her death. She also remembered playing outside whilst lots of old ladies watched from benches around the "women's yard."

During the following week, we took her to visit places she remembered in Beeston, including the Parish Church, Nether Street School, and of course the site of the old Children's Homes, now the Silverwood Nursing Home. On another day, I took her to the Galleries of Justice, the old Nottingham Court House now converted into a museum.

Joan's visit provided a welcome diversion from the normal routine. However, once she returned to Wales, it was time for me to go back to work and also pursue further leads in my search for information about my mother's past.

The death certificate I had ordered for William Arthur Freeman had arrived in the mail and I read its contents with interest. My mother's adoptive father who I had never met died on June 10, 1979, in the University Hospital (QMC), Nottingham, at seventy years of age.

His address at the time of death was given as 162 Long Lane, Attenborough, Nottingham, and the informant was Ivy Muriel Robertson, also of the same address.

Long Lane Attenborough was less than a mile from where I was living and about two miles from Imperial Road, the street where William and Lilian had lived when they adopted my mother. They moved from this house in 1947. Had they always remained in the Beeston area, or had they moved further afield?

Who was Ivy Muriel Robertson, the informant cited on William's death certificate? I was intrigued that she lived at the same address where Lilian Freeman had died in 1972. Could Ivy perhaps be a relative, or possibly a lady friend of William Freeman?

My next port of call was the Nottingham Archives to search through the microfiche records of the Register of Electors. I wanted to ascertain how long William Freeman had lived at Long Lane, Attenborough. Starting in 1979, I became tracing back. I discovered that William had been resident at this address when Lilian died in 1972—and so had Ivy Muriel Robertson.

I continued to trace back through the microfiche records of the Electoral Role. William and Lilian Freeman and Mrs. Robertson had all been residents at 162 Long Lane, Attenborough throughout the 1960s. Now on to the 1950s. On the microfiche for 1959, another name appeared on the Electoral Role. (To comply with the Data Protection Act, I will not use this person's real name but refer to him as Robert.)

There was a reference in brackets before his name [SY]. *S* printed before the elector's name indicated "Service Voter." In other words, this person was a member of one of the armed services. *Y* printed before a name indicated the person would be entitled to vote only at elections held after October 1, 1959. As the age one became eligible to vote at that time was twenty-one, I assumed Robert must have been born around 1938. It seemed Ivy Muriel Robertson had a son.

The names of William Arthur Freeman, Lilian May Freeman, and Ivy Muriel Robertson ceased to appear under this address on the 1950 microfiche. So, it seemed apparent that all three of them had moved into this house together around 1951. How long had

Mrs. Robertson remained after William's death in 1979? This time it was necessary to search the electoral register in the other direction... forwards. I was astonished to discover that Ivy Muriel Robertson remained on the register of electors at this address until 1995!

My next port of call was the local public library. The reason for my visit? To consult the current electoral role. I had made notes of the names of neighbours who lived a few doors either side of William, Lilian, and Ivy and I was curious to know if any of them were still living at Long Lane, Attenborough. I came upon the names of two families who had also been resident since the 1950s and whose names still appeared on the present-day electoral role. They lived next door to each other.

I knew that Ivy Robertson had left this address in 1995. However, Beeston has plenty of retirement complexes and many older people vacate their homes in later life to live in one of these specially adapted flats or bungalows. I hoped that her long-time neighbours might be able to tell me of her present whereabouts, as I would very much have liked to have a conversation with her and ask if the Freemans ever talked about the young girl they had adopted from the Beeston Children's Homes.

Early one evening shortly afterwards, therefore, I knocked on the door of one of these neighbours and made inquiries about Ivy Robertson. "Do you mean Molly?" they asked. I concluded this must have been the name Mrs. Robertson was commonly known by. Sadly, they informed me that she had died in 1995. I then went on to ask about Arthur and Lilian Freeman, and they soon involved their neighbour, an elderly lady, in the conversation.

Yes, they did remember Mr. Freeman very well—such a nice man. Oh yes, and Mrs. Freeman, she had died ages ago. There was some scandal way back, one neighbour mentioned, but she had long forgotten what that was all about. Mr. and Mrs. Freeman had never seemed much of a couple, the other neighbour volunteered. I gathered from these comments that the nature of the relationship between Arthur, Lilian, and "Molly" had at times been the subject of gossip and conjecture amongst the neighbours. I asked if Mrs. Robertson had a son. Yes, he had been a soldier in the army and had married a local girl who had lived further down the street, literally the "girl next door."

What relation did I think the Freemans were to me? Grandparents? No, that could not be the case because the Freemans had no children of their own. I told them that they had adopted a girl, who was my mother, but neither of them knew anything about that. I thanked them for their help and bid them good night.

I now searched back in the microfiche records of deaths at the Family History Centre in West Bridgford for the exact date of Mrs. Robertson's death and sent for a copy of her death certificate. She had been born in June 1912 and died in May 1995 at eighty-two years of age. Her occupation was given as private secretary (retired). The informant was her son Robert (name changed to comply with data protection) and his usual address was given.

It was now 2002. Seven years had gone by since Mrs. Robertson's death. Could her son still be living at the same address as cited on her death certificate? It was certainly possible. In any case, it was worth giving it a try. I penned the following letter dated September 25, 2002.

> Dear Mr. —
>
> *It has not been an easy decision to write to you, and I hope my letter will be favorably received, although it is on rather a sensitive subject.*
>
> *Perhaps it would be best if you read the enclosed article which appeared in the Nottingham Evening Post of 9th September last before you continue to read this letter.*
>
> *As you will have gathered from that article, I learned just over a year ago that my estranged mother committed suicide in 1985. I had not seen her since 1971, shortly before she remarried, and I had been telling myself for years that I should try to contact her again but had kept putting it off. Then when her eldest sister Joan traced me and we started to search in earnest, we found that we were 17 years too late. My feelings of sadness and guilt since then have been unrelenting.*

As the article explains, I have been trying to piece together the details of my mother's life in an attempt to know and understand her better. It turns out that the couple who adopted her in 1945 were William Arthur and Lilian May Freeman, with whom you appear to have had a very close association. Your late mother Ivy Muriel Robertson in fact lived with them (or them with her) for many years at Long Lane, Attenborough. I therefore wonder whether they ever spoke of my mother and why the adoption was so short-lived? Perhaps they hadn't anticipated how difficult it would be for a child brought up almost all her life in an institution to adapt to any other sort of life at 13 years of age.

To be honest with you, until recently, Joan and I thought that the Freemans were foster parents to Mary and didn't realize that they fully and legally adopted her. I suspect that the trustees of the Children's Home and the Nottingham Council had their own plans for the home at that time and were encouraging local people to adopt children without fully discussing with them what a serious commitment this really was. It would not surprise me if some sort of financial incentive was even offered. This may sound rather paranoid, but after all this was the same time that children were being shipped abroad as child migrants by all the major children's charities without the knowledge or consent of their parents, so it does make you wonder.

My motive in making these inquiries is not to blame anyone. This all happened a very long time ago, and everyone involved is now dead. What is done can't be undone, as they say. However, I know I shall not be able to reach closure on this and move on until I have discovered as much as it is possible to know about my mother and the circumstances of her childhood. Please accept my sincere apologies if this letter upsets you or brings up painful memories. I only hope that you can appreciate the distress which I have experienced this past year and my need to try to make sense of it all...

Surprisingly, a few days after I had posted my letter, a reply arrived through my letterbox. It was dated September 29, 2002.

I was most impressed and very moved by the frank and open way Ivy's son Robert replied to my letter. In many ways, it only confirmed information which I already knew; for example, that William Freeman had died in 1979 and Lilian Freeman in 1972. However, it also gave me some insight into where the Freemans initially moved to when they left their rented terraced house on Imperial Road in 1947. William had been a foundry worker at the Beeston Boiler Company. According to Robert's letter, he left there to become a senior partner in a firm which had premises in a millhouse on an island in the River Derwent. It seemed the Freemans had taken a significant step up in the world, and I could not help pondering how this sudden change in fortunes had come about?

There were many unoccupied rooms in the mill, so William and Lilian lived on the premises, and after Ivy Robertson got a job as a secretary in 1949, she also moved in along with her son. The firm was taken over in 1951, and this meant all four of them lost their accommodation. A decision was then made to move to Attenborough and jointly share the house on Long Lane.

Robert continued to live with his mother and the Freemans until he joined the army in 1953 as a young man. However, he saw William and Lilian when returning on leave to visit his mother and says that they always treated him with kindness, and he called them aunt and uncle up until their respective deaths.

He was very surprised to discover that the Freemans had an adopted daughter. He had heard the name Audrey mentioned from time to time, usually when Lilian's brother Alec Thursby and his wife visited. The conversations usually ran along the lines of Audrey showing ingratitude by not keeping in touch, and Robert assumed that Audrey must have been Alec's daughter. He had never seen any photographs of her.

Robert thought that possibly the adoption did not work out because Mrs. Freeman had chronic asthma and could be very demanding when suffering an attack, expecting to be waited on hand and foot. He thought that it would have been difficult for a teenage girl to get on with Mrs. Freeman, as she "was far too self-interested and everything revolved around her needs." However, Mr. Freeman "was a kind and tolerant man but was totally subservient to Lilian's wishes and needs which revolved around her poor health."

In a reply to Robert's letter, I told him that my mother had been very accustomed to carrying out domestic chores whilst living at the Beeston Children's Homes, so I did not think she would leave the Freeman household on that account but rather her stated reason for absconding was that Mr. Freeman had started to interfere with her sexually. Robert has told me that he finds this "very difficult to believe, as it is completely out of character of the man he knew for more than twenty years."

I sincerely hope that he was right. Her adoption by the Freemans was the only opportunity my mother had, in the few years of childhood remaining to her, to experience what it meant to be part of a family. She was at a very vulnerable stage of her life, just entering puberty, so the possibility that Mr. Freeman may have taken advantage of his position of trust as her adoptive father is sickening for me to contemplate.

The fact remains, however, that soon after she became a wife and mother, it was apparent that Audrey was a very mentally and emotionally damaged person, who displayed what are now known to be classic behaviors associated with survivors of child abuse. I therefore believe she must have been a victim at some point in her childhood, although it is impossible now to state categorically when, where, or by whom or the nature and extent of the abuse.

The lack of commitment which the Freemans seem to have had to their decision to adopt Audrey is of concern to me. It seems any relationship William and Lilian may have had with their adoptive daughter had irretrievably broken down after only two years or possibly less. William Arthur Freeman was a relatively young man when the adoption took place. At thirty-five years of age, he was twenty-two years older than my mother. His thirty-eight-year-old wife suffered from poor health and had a tendency to be self-interested

Sometime later, I came into email contact with Ronald Thursby, Lilian Freeman's nephew. He told me that the mill house and factory were situated at Church Wilne, just outside Draycott, Derbyshire. The company, which was called Freeman Glew Limited, manufactured fireworks.

Later still, I discovered from archived newspaper reports that in 1949/50, William Arthur Freeman and three other directors of the firm were prosecuted after it was discovered that they only had a license to manufacture toy caps and sparklers but had actually been manufacturing far more powerful fireworks. It was reported in the Derby Daily Telegraph of January 10, 1950, that "there had been a complete disregard of the most obvious safety precautions."

As a consequence, one man, surname Titherington, was involved in an accident on August 12, 1949, and later died from his injuries. When it came to court, three of the directors, including William Freeman, got off with very nominal fines and one went to prison for a few months. Freeman Glew Limited went into liquidation after that and the business premises were taken over by Haley and Weller Limited, who also manufactured fireworks.

Women, some very young, were also employed at the factory. Ironically, if my mother had not run away from her adoptive parents when she was fifteen years of age and before they moved to Church Wilne to embark on this new business venture, she may well have found herself working for her adoptive father William Arthur Freeman in this very factory.

Hopefully, the Freemans offered to adopt my future mother with good intent, but did they really appreciate what a serious decision this was, the weight of responsibility it placed upon them, and the sacrifices they may need to make in putting the child's interests before their own?

Had anyone sat down with William and Lilian and discussed these issues at length, so that an informed decision could be made as to whether they, as a couple, were suitable to adopt a thirteen year old girl and whether this was in the child's best interests?

I hoped that seeing my mother's adoption file would quieten my growing concerns.

CHAPTER 13
Before the Family Court Judge

ON OCTOBER 15, 2002, I made my way home from work as usual, but tonight a feeling of frustration and despair seemed to be engulfing me. What more could I do? Five weeks had passed since my article had appeared in the *Nottingham Evening Post* and letters had been sent to key people. I had played my "trump card," but my opponent had still not shown their hand. Where did I go from here?

There was a letter waiting for me from Notts County Council Social Services. I opened it and read the contents with some trepidation.

It informed me that the family court judge had now located my mother's adoption records. He was willing to make an exception in my circumstances and allow me to see the file for one hour in his presence at the County Court. I was to telephone his secretary Samantha to arrange a suitable date.

For many, many months I had been fighting for this opportunity. Now a letter was in front of me, confirming at last that my mother's adoption records still existed and that I could see them. Why did I feel no sense of elation?

Firstly, I deeply resented the way I had been treated. If an adopted person wishes to obtain a copy of their birth certificate and see their adoption records, there is an official process in place to allow them to do this, and they receive a visit from a social worker and counseling to help them appreciate what the implications of accessing this information might mean, the emotional trauma it may trigger and so forth. In contrast, I was made to feel that I was being granted some huge concession in being allowed to see my mother's adoption file. Also, no one seemed to be giving any thought to the emotional trauma I might experience as a result. There was to be no counseling beforehand, no social worker present who understood the issues that persons affected by adoption might grapple with to give support. I was to be granted the concession of seeing my mother's adoption records for one hour at the County Court in the presence of a judge. I expressed my feelings in a letter to Pam Hodgkins of NORCAP, dated October 23, 2002.

> ...I suppose this is a victory for me, but to be perfectly honest, I feel very nervous about it because an hour is such a short period of time, and I am worried that I won't be able to absorb all the information.
>
> I also feel very intimidated that I have to examine these in the presence of a Judge. I know of adopted people who have requested to see their own adoption records, and they have been assisted by specially trained social workers and counselors who have supported them through this process. In contrast, I feel as though I'm being cast in the role of a troublemaker who is wasting everybody's time, and that they are doing me a huge favour by letting me see information relating to my own mother! In reality, this is a very emotive subject for me and the past 18 months have been the most emotionally traumatic time of my life. I feel that I could do with some empathy and support, but very much doubt I'll get it. I wonder whether I will be allowed to ask any questions, or take notes, or whether I am allowed to take anyone with me, but I don't feel free to ask any of these questions. However, after putting so much effort in to persuade them, I certainly don't want to pass this opportunity up, so I will certainly go along...

It was imperative I put these issues to one side. When I visited the county court, my mind must be totally focused on my purpose for being there—to see my mother's adoption records and assimilate as much information as possible in just one hour.

I telephoned the county court, and an appointment was made for November 8. On the day I made my way there in torrential rain, and on my arrival, I was greeted by Samantha. What a pleasant young lady she turned out to be. I felt immediately at ease in her presence. She told me that Ms. P of Notts County Council Social Services had said that if she were intending to be present at my meeting with the judge, there would be no need for a social worker from the council to come along. I resented their disinterest, but Samantha had such a kind and reassuring manner that I began to feel glad that she would be there instead.

After leading me up a flight of stairs and along several corridors, Samantha stopped at a door and, after knocking, ushered me in. The judge was a slightly built man, and as I was introduced to him, I sensed he was a little nervous, which surprised me. I was nervous too, but I am quite good at hiding it. He had been sitting in court that morning and was to return after this break for the afternoon session but had thankfully dispensed with his wig and gown for our meeting. A tray of tea/coffee had been set up and Samantha offered me a drink, which I accepted.

"Would you like a drink, Your Honour?" When speaking to the judge, Samantha always referred to him very respectfully as "Your Honour."

His Honour asked me where I worked, which I personally thought was a bit odd but perhaps he was just trying to make me feel at ease. He told me that he was currently in charge of all adoptions in the Nottingham area. The conversation then turned to my mother's adoption and how Samantha had found the file in the archives. His Honour commented on the dearth of information contained in adoption files from that era (1940s) compared to today. I asked, as respectfully as I could, if the file I was going to see contained all the information that had originally been in it or whether they had felt they should withhold any documents. Samantha assured me nothing had been removed. During this conversation she also made reference to my article in the *Nottingham Evening Post* and said that the Council had forwarded the article on to the county court. So, all my efforts in writing that article and getting it published had achieved something! It had possibly influenced the decision in favour of me being allowed access to my mother's adoption file, as I had hoped it would.

His Honour asked what I hoped to achieve by seeing the file, and I began to wonder whether, depending on my answer, he may still decide against letting me have access. I said that I didn't really know what it would achieve, if anything, but that I felt strongly that I should be allowed to see it.

He then brought the file over and asked if I felt "ready for this." I commented that I had already been to the coroner's office and looked through the file containing, among other things, the inquest report into my mother's suicide and that nothing in this file could be more upsetting than that.

His Honour brought the file over and stood by me, turning the pages and pointing out various documents and what they meant. I was surprised at how much was in there. There were various green forms, which I believe are called "Consent of Adoption" or ACA.2, quite a number of certificates, including her adoptive parents' respective birth and marriage certificates, her actual parents' birth certificates, and her mother's death certificate (she died of TB at thirty-seven years of age in 1933 when my mother was one year nine months old). His Honour pointed out a document signed by the Freeman's undertaking to feed, clothe, and support my mother. I said that as she was leaving school in five months' time from the date of the adoption, they wouldn't have to do that for very long.

At the back was a short guardian ad litem's report on my mother's history. It said she had been a resident at the Children's Home since a very young age. Mr. and Mrs. Freeman had been married twelve years and had no children of their own. His Honour pointed out several times that, according to the guardian ad litem's report, my mother had spent some holidays with the Freemans prior to the adoption and had expressed a desire to live with them permanently. I said that I was puzzled as to why, in that case, they hadn't adopted her years earlier, which would have saved her from spending almost her entire childhood in an institution.

After we had been through the file in this way, the judge asked if I had seen everything I needed to see. I had been told I could see the file between 1:00 to 2:00 p.m. It was now 1:40pm and His Honour was expected back in court. Samantha told the judge that she was happy to remain with me if I wanted to look at the file for longer, but he seemed reluctant to agree to this. I did, however, say that I would like to quickly look through it again and make a couple of notes.

At this point, the telephone rang and the judge was pre-occupied in answering it for a few minutes. I was grateful for this respite, as I had found it quite intimidating and distracting having him standing right behind me, pointing things out in the file.

One question which I had particularly wanted the answer to was whether my mother's father had given his permission for the adoption to take place, and he had indeed signed the ACA.2 Consent to Adoption form. However, on looking through the file a second time, I noticed that the signature beneath his (as witness) was that of his son and my mother's brother, John Edwin Green. By this time, the judge had finished his telephone call and came over to stand behind me once again. I pointed to the two signatures on the form and explained that the person who had witnessed Walter Edwin Green's signature in the capacity of Clerk to Messrs. Acton, Marriott and Simpson was, in fact, his own son and my mother's brother. His Honor seemed a little puzzled by this. I explained that Mr. Simpson was a Trustee of the Children's Home and had employed John Green as a junior clerk when he left school. The other two signatories to the ACA.2 were a judge and Mr. Simpson himself.

The fact that both her father and her brother signed the consent form for my mother's adoption out of their family upset me considerably because it seemed like a double betrayal to me. I was of the understanding that John had gone into the navy in 1943 and was no longer in the employ of Messrs. Acton, Marriott and Simpson. Perhaps I have the dates wrong or perhaps he was home on leave at the time. Was it actually legal for someone so young to be a signatory on an official document such as this?

In any case, this explained why John could inform his sister Joan with such confidence when she traced him in 1999 after fifty-six years that their sister Mary was no longer of the family, as she had been adopted, and therefore had no right to share in their late sister Dorothy's estate.

After our interview, His Honor instructed Samantha to return my mother's file to the archives and commented that hopefully it would never need to see the light of day again. However, as she was showing me out, Samantha told me that she would keep the file on her desk for the next week in case I thought of any further questions I wanted to ask. I was grateful for her kindness.

I had hoped that seeing my mother's adoption file would finally help me to come to terms with all that had happened and free me to move on. However, if anything I felt more deeply troubled than ever before.

The guardian ad litem's report, submitted by William Noel Parr of Friary Chambers in August 1944, was so general that I seriously doubted that this person had ever met the Freemans or the thirteen-year-old child they wished to adopt. He certainly never mentioned having interviewed them or visited their house or spoken to my mother. It was written in the third person and contained very general information, which Mr. Parr could have easily obtained third hand, possibly through Mr. Simpson. The whole report seemed to be written in the spirit of merely going through the legalities required by the 1926 Adoption Act rather than in the spirit of ascertaining what was really in the best interests of the child involved.

I also found it so hurtful that both my mother's father and her brother had signed the ACA.2 Consent to Adoption Form. I could not comprehend how Mr. Simpson had been so heartless or thoughtless or both to ask John to do this. Did he imagine that John would have been able to influence his father to sign the form more readily, perhaps reassuring him that this course of action was for the best. Had they all met together in Mr. Simpson's office and discussed this decision in some depth, or had John merely visited his father with the form and obtained his signature? There is probably only one person who could answer that question, and that is John Edwin Green himself. How ironic that this piece of paper, signed by John on November 30, 1944, and constituting his sister Mary as "no longer of the family" would ensure that, fifty-five years later, John received an additional £60,000 (£180,000 instead of £120,000) when Dorothy's estate was split two ways instead of three.

What of George Thornton Simpson? Was he a saint or a sinner? He had been a trustee of the Beeston Children's Homes since as far back as 1922, a time when poverty and wealth, hardship and privilege co- existed, and the upper classes considered it their duty, as pillars of the community, to be charitable to the poor and needy? In 1925, the annual report for the Homes listed four Trustees: G. Thornton Simpson, Esq.; O. W. Hind, Esq.; Sir H. D. Readett-Bayley; and F. H. Starling, Esq.

The Homes could boast of Committee members from amongst the "great and the good," namely:-

Mrs. J. C. Boot, Mrs. J. D. Player, Ms. Bright, Mrs. W. R. Smith, Mrs. Greenshield Davis, Ms. Tawse, Mrs. Fisk, Mrs. Turner, Mrs.

R. Granger, Ms. Turney, Mrs. O. W. Hind, Lady Jacoby, Mrs. E.W. Paul. In addition, Mr. G. Thornton Simpson was also the honorary treasurer and Mrs. G. Thornton Simpson the honorary secretary.

However, by 1947, George Thornton Simpson was one of only two remaining active trustees of the Children's Homes and times were changing. The Second World War had just ended, and the world would never be the same again. Britain had come off victorious against Nazi Germany but had paid dearly. Thousands had made the "supreme sacrifice," leaving widows and orphans in abundance. Britain's economy had been stretched to breaking point, and now the country must fight to get back on its feet. Although they may not have admitted it, even to themselves, many had inwardly lost their belief in the old values.

So, if presented with the opportunity to benefit personally from money given by a wealthy widow for the benefit of the poor and disadvantaged, could George Thornton Simpson, this respectable professional gentleman, be tempted or was he merely the victim of a chance set of circumstances, which hindered his attempts to make a most generous gesture by gifting the Children's Homes to the local authority? Perhaps, after over twenty-five years' involvement with the Homes, Mr. Simpson felt he deserved to get something out of it, and maybe he was right!

On a more personal note, Mr. Simpson had certainly been a benefactor to my uncle, John Green, giving him the opportunity to start a career in the legal profession by taking him on as a junior clerk at Messrs. Acton, Marriott and Simpson when he left school in 1942 at fourteen years of age. When Mr. Simpson arranged my mother's adoption in 1945, did he likewise have her best interests at heart, or was she a victim of a ruthless policy to greatly reduce the amount of children resident at the Homes so that the takeover by the Notts Corporation could go ahead smoothly without the need to relocate too many children?

Ultimately, it comes down to motives. If George Thornton Simpson's motives were sincere, if he truly believed he was acting in the best interests of the children concerned, then he is a saint. If he was acting for his own benefit, whether to enhance his reputation and standing in the community, appear benevolent, or benefit financially, then he is a sinner.

Truth be known, most of us do things for more or less the right reasons but probably hope to get some payoff at the end of the day. So, saint or sinner? Only God can be the judge of our motives, as the scriptures tell us:

"There is nothing that can be hidden from God; everything in all creation is exposed and lies open before his eyes. And it is to him that we must all give an account of ourselves" (Hebrews 4:13 GNB).

Following my meeting with the judge, I penned the following letter dated November 16, 2002, which reads, in part:

> *Your Honour*
>
> *Firstly, I would like to express my thanks to you for allowing me to come to the Court on 8 November and access my deceased mother's adoption records...*
>
> *I had hoped that accessing my mother's adoption file would help me to draw a line under the last 18 months and finally move on, and during our meeting, I sensed that you were anxious to reassure me that my mother's late adoption was perfectly open and above board and in her best interests. However, I'm afraid that, although several questions which had been troubling me were answered by seeing the adoption file, if anything its contents raised even greater concerns in my mind.*
>
> *I had wondered whether her father gave his permission for the adoption to take place, and indeed he had signed the ACA.2 Consent of Adoption form. This was no great surprise to me. Joan had informed me that their father was a drunkard and a womanizer, and as he had taken no responsibility for or interest in his four children after the death of their mother in 1933, why should he want to retain parental rights over his youngest daughter now? However, it did surprise and upset me that John Edwin Green, his son and my mother's brother, signed underneath to witness his father's signature...*
>
> *Joan is also very upset about this. My mother had two sisters, Joan and Dorothy, both older than John.*
>
> *Why were they not informed of their sister's adoption? Joan traced John in 1999 after the death of their sister Dorothy,*

and it came as such a shock when he told her not to bother trying to find Mary because she had been adopted and was therefore "no longer of the family" and not entitled to inherit anything under Dorothy's will.

I am also very concerned about the superficial nature of the Guardian Ad Litem's report. As you pointed out, it does make mention of the fact that my mother had spent some holidays from the Children's Homes with the Freemans prior to the adoption, and that she was agreeable to living with them permanently (and presumably to assuming the name Lilian Audrey Freeman, after being Gladys Mary Green for 13 years). However, the fact that Mrs. Lilian Freeman was a chronically sick woman seems to have been completely overlooked.

…I am therefore giving serious consideration to seeking legal advice in this matter. It is my wish to have what I believe to be the totally unnecessary and ill-advised adoption of my mother posthumously annulled. Although the Freemans may have thought they were acting in a benevolent and noble way in adopting my mother, they actually did her a great disservice, as is evident from the short time she lived with them, during which she was at best a skivvy and at worst possibly sexually abused. Her adoption made a travesty of everything that adoption should stand for…

In conclusion, even if I seek legal advice and am told that it is impossible to get the adoption annulled, it will still mean a great deal to me to have been able to see my mother's adoption records, and once again I want to thank you for making that possible for me.

Aware of the large amount of money which Aunt Joan had paid out in legal fees, and the fact that my financial resources were very limited, I was rather hesitant about involving a solicitor. However, a partner at Actons solicitors quoted a very reasonable fixed fee to investigate the matter and meet with me to discuss the possibility of having Audrey's adoption posthumously annulled.

In a letter dated January 31, 2003, he summarized his findings. The salient points are as follows:-

> *...I write to confirm my view that it will not be possible to successfully pursue an application for the annulment of your mother's adoption.*

The solicitor cited several relevant cases and then continued:

> *The principle that emerges from these cases is that the order can only be set aside if it is the natural parents who have suffered an injustice so that there has not been a proper and valid consent to the adoption. I am afraid that I cannot conceive of a case being allowed to proceed therefore where the application is brought solely in the child's interests, particularly once the child has reached its majority and certainly after the child has died.*

Following this advice, I decided there was no point in me trying to pursue a posthumous annulment of the adoption order.

It is beyond doubt that my mother's short-term adoption has had very long-term consequences. It is impossible, of course, to calculate the high emotional cost that has been exacted, but no one can dispute the loss materially. As I further said in my letter to the judge:

> *...It is impossible to prove that my mother would have been any happier or coped better as a mother if the Freemans had not adopted her. However, when Joan started searching for her long-lost brother and sister in 1999, it was because she wanted them to share in their deceased sister Dorothy's estate. Dorothy, who never married or had children, left £360,000 after deduction of inheritance tax. Under the intestacy laws, if my mother had not been adopted, she would have been entitled to a third of that. In the event of her death, her share would pass to her children.*

> *In other words, looking at it from a purely material point of view which can be calculated, because of her adoption I have lost out on £120,000.*

I suppose if money were no object, and you could afford to hire a brilliant legal team, it might be possible to make a precedent of this case. For example, several years after Audrey's adoption took place, legal amendments were made which altered her entitlement in the event of an intestacy. (See points 5–10 of Andrew P. D. Walker's advice in chapter 14.)

One could challenge the fairness of these amendments as they relate to this particular case, but how much would it cost to successfully argue the point and get the law rewritten?

Likely more than I could ever afford to pay.

CHAPTER 14
Rage, Rage Against the Dying of the Light

AUNT JOAN HAD ACCEPTED MY offer to travel down to London with her to consult with a barrister on the matter of initiating proceedings in the Chancery Division to prove Dorothy's will in solemn form. She felt this was the only recourse left to her now that the negotiations with her brother John to voluntarily return a third of the monies he had received from their late sister Dorothy's estate for the benefit of Mary's daughters had broken down.

Joan's solicitors had already consulted Andrew P. D. Walker, a barrister, on a previous occasion. This was during the administration of Dorothy's estate, and he was asked to advise regarding the rights of Gladys Mary Green. His note of advice dated February 2, 2000, concluded, in part:

5. I must assume for present purposes that Gladys was adopted pursuant to an adoption order under the Adoption of Children Act 1926. That would appear to be the case from the formal entry of the word "Adopted" on her birth certificate, but the full circumstances are unknown.

6. An adoption under the Adoption of Children Act 1926 did not itself affect the rights on any intestacy which an adopted child would have had if the adoption order had not been made: s.5(2)" *

Adoption of Children Act, 1926 – Section 5(2) states:

"An adoption order shall not deprive the adopted child of any right to or interest in property to which, but for the order, the child would have been entitled under any intestacy or disposition, whether occurring or made before or after the making of the adoption order, or confer on the adopted child any right to or interest in property as a child of the adopter...The rights of adopted children were changed, however, in respect of all deaths or dispositions after 1 January 1950; this change will apply to Dorothy's death. The change was, in essence, to treat an adopted child on intestacy as the natural child of her adoptive parents, and as not being the child of anyone else.

7. The effect of that change so far as Dorothy's estate is concerned, is that Gladys (Mary) became entitled to rights as if she were the natural child of her adoptive parent(s), but lost her rights as the sister of Dorothy.

8. That change has been reflected in the various changes in legislation since 1949, and the key aspect of this is now enshrined in sections 38(1) (b), 39(2), and 39(5) (a) of the Adoption Act 1976.

9. As a result, Dorothy's estate is to be distributed without reference to the existence of Gladys (Mary), so will fall to be distributed equally between Joan and John under ss.46(1)(v) and 47 of the Administration of Estates Act 1925.

Andrew Walker then went on to give various suggestions as to how Joan and John might protect themselves against possible future claims from Gladys Mary or her children to a third share in Dorothy's estate, if the adoption were found not to be legally binding. However, a search company, acting under instructions from Joan's solicitor, seemed to have established beyond reasonable doubt that Gladys Mary Green had indeed been legally adopted. Copies of her birth certificate (marked "Adopted" in the right-hand margin), and her adoption certificate had been obtained, along with her two marriage certificates.

Interestingly, on the certificate relating to her marriage to my father in 1951, under the column for father's name and surname, Mary has cited William Arthur Freeman (adoptive parent). However, on the certificate pertaining to her later marriage to Herbert Goodwin in 1972, she cites Edward Green (deceased) as her paternal father. This surely shows that she had long since ceased to consider the Freemans as her "parents" in any respect, if indeed she ever had.

Messrs. H and P therefore released the monies from Dorothy's estate to Joan and John in equal shares in March 2000, although Joan adamantly maintains that she, as administratrix, never expressly agreed to this. It was her wish that, adoption or no adoption, she and John should agree, before the money was released, to reserve a third share for Mary in the event that she or her children could be traced. It seems reasonable to conclude that, if Messrs. H and P had not released the monies until agreement had been reached between Joan and John, Joan would have been in a much stronger position to negotiate a settlement which conformed to her wishes. Once £180,000, half of Dorothy's estate, was electronically transferred into his bank account, John would, naturally, be far less inclined to cooperate with what he saw as Joan's sentimental notion of tracing their youngest sister and including her in their good fortune.

Having said that, I think it is only fair to acknowledge John Green's side of the matter.

It transpires that during the year it took to administer Dorothy's estate, and before relations between them completely broke down, there was a telephone conversation between Joan and her brother John when Joan said something which intimated that she, and not Dorothy, had destroyed the will. John was greatly concerned about this, and on June 30 he telephoned Joan's solicitor, asking them to probe into matters further.

On July 1, 1999, Joan was contacted by her solicitor, and said that she had been drinking prior to the telephone conversation with John and was therefore not very coherent. She could not remember saying that she had torn the will up. Joan was asked directly by her solicitor whether she had done so. Joan said she had not. (Perhaps Joan did not consider that she was telling an outright lie because she later claimed that Terence Carter, a neighbour of Dorothy's, had torn it up after she instructed him to do so.) It was explained to Joan that as Duncan Worsley had died, under the terms of the will, she would have been the sole beneficiary.

Joan still allowed her solicitor to believe that the will was already ripped up when found, presumably by Dorothy, which would invalidate it.

Messrs. H and P therefore telephoned John and reassured him that Joan had categorically denied ripping up Dorothy's will. Following this assurance, both parties agreed that the estate should continue to be administered on the basis of an intestacy. Shortly after this, both Joan and John were offered an interim payment of £30,000 each from the estate. John returned his cheque, stating that he would rather wait until the whole matter had been settled. It was another eight months before the estate was finally distributed, during which time Joan could have come forward at any time and confessed. However, she did not do so until shortly after the monies were released. The frustration this must have caused her brother John therefore has to be acknowledged. His legal representative, in a letter sent to Joan's solicitor dated June 19, 2002, summed it up:

"(Joan) does not appear to appreciate the gravity of her actions and statements, the inconvenience, upset and worry she has caused to our client and the potential legal and tax minefield she has created."

Still, here we were on our way down to London to consult a barrister, in hopes of being able to rectify the situation. We were ushered into a room where the walls were lined with bookcases and filled with legal volumes from top to bottom. We sat at a large wooden table, Aunt Joan and I on one side, her solicitor and the female barrister the other.

The barrister, Ms. Reed, had read up on the case extensively and acknowledged it was a very "sad story." At this point, Joan was asked very pointedly to confirm whether or not she had ripped the will up. She hesitated for a moment and asked whether she had to be "absolutely truthful." She was told that, of course, she must, and I wondered what was coming. It was at this point that Joan confessed that Terence Carter had ripped the will up, but on her instructions. Ms. Reed had already been in touch with Terence Carter about possibly being a witness in court on Joan's behalf, and he had not been too keen at the prospect. This was perhaps understandable, as what Joan now claimed directly contradicted a former statement which she and Terence Carter made, in which they both claimed that Joan had torn up the will.

I asked whether, if the case came to court, it would be explained that Joan had tried for an extensive period of time to settle matters amicably with her brother by reaching an agreement to return just one third, or £60,000, of the total amount he had received? It was explained that because John had prefaced all his letters "without prejudice," reference could not be made to their contents in court. I further asked whether the circumstances of my mother's unhappy childhood, her disastrous adoption, and subsequent suicide would be taken into consideration. It was explained that this was unlikely, as the court would be dealing strictly with the matter of the validity or otherwise of Dorothy's will.

Ms. Reed stressed it was crucial to Joan's case that John Green agree, if the court acknowledged the validity of the will, to voluntarily return the monies that he had received. In her opinion, there was little point in bringing the case to court unless he would agree to this beforehand. There was a basis for believing that he would agree, as in a letter dated May 21, 2000, addressed to Joan's solicitor and in reply to their letter informing him that the will was valid and he should therefore return the money, he had stated: *"...I would not wish to receive or retain monies to which I was not entitled."*

Joan agreed that John should be approached in the first instance, to see if he still held to this view. Following that, she said she would "be guided by the advice of my nieces". I could only chuckle at that statement and remarked, "Well, that'll be a first!" as Joan has never, to my knowledge, taken Jill's or my advice on any matter.

After leaving Ms. Reed's chambers, Joan and I went to have a cup of tea in a café before catching our respective trains for the journey home. I was very disappointed with the outcome of the conference, as I felt that the moral issues which really mattered to me would not be addressed, even if the case came to court.

"You know, Aunt Joan, you may just have to accept that you made a very, very costly mistake," I remarked. However, I don't think Joan was of a mind to listen.

Following our conference, Messrs. H and P wrote to John via his solicitor on September 30, 2002:

"Our client is preparing to issue proceedings in the Chancery Division to prove the Will in solemn form. We are instructed to write to enquire whether your client will agree that if our client proves the Will in solemn form, and agrees to pay your client's costs of the same...your client will agree that the Estate should be administered in accordance with the Will and that he will refund the monies received by him in March 2000..."

Messrs. I. R. G. replied on November 15, 2002, once again specifically requesting a reply to their letter of July 22, 2002, when they had asked that Joan give an explanation for what appeared to be very irrational behavior during the period of the administration (of the estate), "so that our client can give further consideration to his position."

Messrs. H and P replied on November 19, 2002, once again stating, "Our client will not be providing any further explanations as requested in your letter of July 22, 2002."

I considered this request perfectly reasonable, and therefore Joan and I had compiled a statement dated July 30, 2002, explaining the reasons for her actions as honestly as we could. Joan had signed this statement and forwarded it to Messrs. H and P. However, they had never sent it on to John's solicitor, maintaining that it would be prejudicial to Joan's case.

In any event, John Green had by this time consulted a barrister himself, and on December 10, 2002, his solicitor replied to Messrs. H and P, making the following salient points:

1. Even if your Client claims to be an unsatisfied legatee, our Client cannot be compelled to refund what he has received "if the assets be originally sufficient to satisfy all legatees...because the payment was not a devastivat in the Executor and because the legatee who received payment is protected by the principle that "vigilantibus non dormientibus jure subvenieunt"—see re Diplock [1948] 1 Ch 465 @ 483-484.

2. Your Client may not recover an overpayment if she was the person responsible for the mistake that was made—

3. As your Client made the payment to our Client voluntarily (i.e. not under compulsion of proceedings) it is presumed

that your Client had sufficient assets to pay all legacies and she would only be able to compel our Client to refund what he has received if liabilities appear of which your Client had no notice—see Jervis -v- Wolfestan (1874) LR 18 Eq 18.

The above three points basically meant that even if Joan succeeded in getting the court to recognize the will as valid, she only had a slim chance of recovering any monies already paid to John. This is why her barrister Ms. Reed had stated so adamantly that Joan should only pursue the case in court if John was prepared to agree beforehand that he would voluntarily return his share of the estate should the will be proved in solemn form.

There was no point in Joan pursuing what was certain to be an extremely protracted and costly court case under these circumstances, and in a letter dated December 19, 2002, Joan's solicitor wrote, "…as your brother is not prepared at this stage to agree that if the Will is proved that he will repay the money, you have decided not to pursue the matter of the existence of the will any further. I know that this is a difficult thing for you to do but feel that it is really the only option as you are unlikely to receive any benefit from any proceedings and in fact quite the reverse."

Joan's solicitor continued, "I enclose my firm's final account for your attention…I have written to (John's solicitor) confirming that you will not be proceeding further in relation to Dorothy's estate and that my firm is no longer instructed."

This letter was written without a final consultation with Joan, and we both got the impression that Messrs. H and P were hastily trying to extract themselves from what had become an extremely messy situation. Joan had paid out thousands of pounds in legal fees yet had achieved absolutely nothing.

Joan had finally come to the end of the line in trying to resolve the matter legally, and this was a bitter pill for her to swallow. I hoped she would now be able to settle her mind on the matter and simply enjoy building up a relationship with her newly found nieces and our families. It would be nice not to have every telephone conversation with her dominated by "how things were proceeding."

However, Joan has been a fighter all her life, and she could not be gracious in defeat. Having come to the end of the line in fighting the matter legally, she resolved that she would be a "thorn in John's side" until the day she died. After some months, she had a friend's son print out some leaflets for her, berating John and his family. She then took herself down to the Cotswold's town where her brother lived, accompanied by Gina, her little dog, checked herself into a guest house, and spent the next few days distributing the leaflets around the town. She called into a local estate agency to find out the location of the street where her brother lived. When the sales negotiator said that she herself lived on that street, Joan asked if she knew John Green. The lady replied that she did, and that he was a very well- respected member of the community. Needless to say, she got a leaflet and a chance to know Joan's opinion of his character. Joan also left leaflets at the police station, the church, and tied them to the stocks in the Market Square. As she took about forty leaflets in total down with her, presumably the others were distributed indiscriminately around the town.

The leaflet was headed "THIEVES." Underneath was a photograph of John Green, his wife, son and daughter at his son's graduation. In bold capital letters, the text read:

MR. JOHN E. GREEN AND FAMILY
FROM WORKHOUSE TO THE COTSWOLDS

And then continued...

> *He robbed our youngest sister of her inheritance by signing adoption papers. This stopped her getting her rightful share and meaning he got it by default. Her adoption gave her such traumas she sadly committed suicide.*
>
> *They, by knowing the law (their son, a barrister; their daughter, a doctor) have managed to steal their dead sister's inheritance.*
>
> *I am 78 years old, and if I had not traced him, he would not have been found. I have done this because he is callous, greedy, and arrogant and deserves to be shown up.*
>
> *I could have done without this heartache. I hope you good citizens of Stow-on-the-Wolds will forgive me for this*

intrusion. I am the eldest sister, and we lost our mother when we were small children. My address is…

In addition, Joan purchased an aerosol can of paint, went to John's house, and sprayed it on the front door and the windows. She then walked away with her little dog and sat on a bench nearby. John ran after her and confronted her about spraying the paint. "You'd better go and report me to the police then" was Joan's reply. Nothing could have pleased her more than being arrested and charged, as she believed this would give her the opportunity to expose what she considered John's meanness and hard-heartedness in court.

John, however, turned on his heels and returned home, busying himself in an attempt to remove the paint before it dried. Joan returned to the house after dark and sprayed it again before retiring for the night and travelled home the next day.

Once Joan was back home and able to recount her exploits over the telephone, I thought how very sad it was that she and her brother had come face-to-face for the first time in sixty years in such unhappy circumstances. What would their deceased sister Dorothy have made of all this quarreling over her inheritance?

Joan had assured us that her visit would "lance the boil," thereby releasing the bitterness and anger which were bubbling up within her. She was disappointed not to have any feedback regarding the leaflet, even though she had printed her name, address, and telephone number on it. However, we certainly hoped this would now be the end of the matter.

It was, for a while. Then after a few months, Joan asked me if I would be able to trace the whereabouts of John's barrister son on the internet. I refused, of course, because I did not agree with what Joan was doing and didn't want to be a party to it. Joan nevertheless contacted a private detective and found out his whereabouts in a matter of days. He was practicing in barristers' chambers in Temple Gardens, London EC4Y. She rang up requesting to speak to him on several occasions, but he refused to take her calls. She then determined to have another leaflet printed and to go down to London to distribute these outside his chambers. Her friend's son questioned why she needed to do this because the barristers' chambers had a website, and each barrister had a personal email address listed. He therefore offered to distribute the leaflet via email. Once again, it was headed "THIEVES" and read as follows:-

> *D. G., Barrister (name omitted to comply with Data Protection Act), whom along with his father and family have stolen my dead sister's estate, leaving my youngest sister's children without their inheritance. Because of their superior knowledge of the law, they know I am unable to take them to court, as having been to barristers myself they say I could lose my home or go to prison if I lost, As I am 79 years old you can see my hesitation.*
>
> *Because my brother John signed for my young sister to be adopted, he now claims her money. I am sure his son who puts in his portfolio that he specializes in human rights must examine his conscience. It was this unhappy adoption that led to her suicide.*
>
> *He has had the advantage of a good education, but the females of this sorry family have proved their worth and I will try to get justice for them before I die. This is not the end of the matter, as I will find other ways to get justice.*

Once again, Joan had openly put her address and telephone number on the leaflet and was most disappointed that she got no feedback. She did not understand how email worked and began to doubt that anyone had actually received the leaflet. She therefore determined that she would go down to London anyway.

It was now early November, and I tried to encourage her to put her visit off until the spring, as I knew to oppose her outright would only make her more determined. I had a few days annual leave remaining and offered to come to Wales to visit her. However, she was adamant she must go sooner rather than later.

This time her exploits involved entering the very plush offices and demanding to speak with her nephew, D. G. Whilst the clerk went away, presumably to locate him, she set up placards and distributed leaflets in the reception area and tried, unsuccessfully, to fasten herself to a sofa with a lock and chain she had taken for this purpose. Aunt Joan was informed that her barrister nephew was not in chambers but stated that she did not believe that for a moment. A gentleman tried to placate her, offering her a cup of tea, which she declined.

Shortly afterwards, the police arrived. Seeing that her escapade was soon to be curtailed, Joan announced to the police constables, "Stand back please!" following which she poured paint, which she had previously transferred into two bottles, all over the carpet.

Joan was arrested and led out to the police van. Probably on account of her age, the policemen said she had better sit in the front passenger seat. In response to a question from Joan, they acknowledged that she probably was the most senior person they had ever arrested.

At the police station, a mug shot, fingerprints, and a DNA sample were taken, following which Joan was put in a police cell and had to wait five hours before a solicitor could be found to come out and interview her. He turned out to be a young Irishman, who Joan found "absolutely charming." He was very keen to get Joan to admit that she was sorry for her actions. No prizes for guessing Joan's answer to that!

Joan's protest coincided with the exploits of a member of Fathers4Justice, an intrepid group which fights for fathers' rights to have regular access to their children in the event of a breakdown in relations with the mother and what they see as the court's failure to enforce those rights. To draw attention to their plight, the aggrieved father had donned a Spiderman costume, climbed to the top of a crane in the vicinity of Tower Bridge, and remained there for six days. This one-man protest had a devastating effect on the Capital, as the police decided to close Tower Bridge, a major route for motorists crossing the Thames river for several days, resulting in ten-mile traffic jams during the rush hour.

The media reported that Mayor Ken Livingstone was furious, stating that "action has to be taken to allow Londoners to move around the city and not be held to ransom by one individual," adding that the protestor was "amply demonstrating why some men should not have access to their own children."

The arrest and arrival at the Snow Hill police station of a militant senior citizen who had just mounted her own protest in another part of the city coincided with all this mayhem and caused a senior police officer to state that Joan was "the final straw."

Interestingly, the aggrieved father appeared at Southwark Crown Court in May 2004 charged with causing a public nuisance, but after a nine-day trial he was cleared of the charge because his legal representatives successfully argued that the police had closed Tower Bridge of their own volition as a bargaining tool to mount psychological pressure on the man to abandon his protest rather than purely in the interests of public health and safety.

However, back to Aunt Joan. Finally, she was released, and the next day caught the train to make the lengthy journey home to Wales. She had contracted a bad dose of the flu and spent about a week recovering.

Joan had managed to get herself a criminal record but was disappointed that she was not charged, as she was seeking publicity. I constantly worry about what Joan will get up to next and have told her I wish she could be settled about the matter in her own mind and heart, but she adamantly refuses to be a "quiet old lady." Joan agrees with the sentiments expressed by Dylan Thomas in his poem, "Do not go gentle into that good night," and has every intention of following them.

Do Not Go Gentle Into that Good Night

Do not go Gentle into that good night
Old age should burn and rave at close of day;
Rage, rage against the dying of the light

Though wise men at their end know dark is right,
Because their words had forked no lightning they
Do not go gentle into that good night.

Good men, the last wave by, crying how bright
Their frail deeds might have danced in a green bay,
Rage, rage against the dying of the light.

Wild men who caught and sang the sun in flight,
And learn, too late, they grieved it on its way,
Do not go gentle into that good night.

Grave men, near death, who see with blinding sight
Blind eyes could blaze like meteors and be gay,
Rage, rage against the dying of the light.

And you, my father, there on the sad height,
Curse, bless, me now with your fierce tears, I pray.
Do not go gentle into that good night.
Rage, rage against the dying of the light.

Dylan Thomas

CHAPTER 15
The Trail Goes Cold

DURING THE MANY MONTHS of fighting to be allowed to see my mother's adoption records, it struck me forcibly that, in contrast to the struggle I was having, there is actually a legal process in place for adopted persons to obtain their original birth certificates and see their adoption records if they so wish. I had therefore encouraged my sister Jill to ask to see her adoption file. She had always maintained that finding me had provided the link to her birth family, which she had wanted, and that she had no desire to know more or take it any further. However, she appreciated that her own adoption file might actually tell us something important about our mother and for this reason agreed to initiate the process.

A social worker contacted her and arranged to visit. They do not immediately appear with your adoption file, but speak to you and counsel you if needed as to the implications of the step you are taking, and that you may not necessarily be comforted by the information you learn. On this first visit, Jill took the opportunity to explain how our Aunt Joan had contacted us and how it had become apparent that we actually knew very little about our mother's past, particularly her childhood. She showed the social worker the newspaper article which had appeared in the *Nottingham Evening Post*, and told him how I had finally been allowed to see my mother's adoption records, but only for an hour in the presence of a judge at the county court, with no prior counseling or support from a qualified social worker, and that I was very unhappy about the way I had been treated.

The social worker (who asked not to be named) was appalled at this. They said that, in view of what had happened, they would be happy for me to be there on the next visit, if that would help. The next time the social worker came to Jill's house, it was with copies of her adoption records for her to keep.

As hoped, we did learn a little more about our mother from the guardian ad litem's report pertaining to Jill's adoption. It stated:-

The mother of the infant, with her two elder sisters, was placed in a Children's Home at birth, following her mother's death. She was adopted at the age of 11, but absconded from home at the age of 15, going into lodgings. She met her present husband at this time. A year after her marriage she attempted to commit suicide and was admitted to Mapperley Hospital. A series of breakdowns followed, and she tried a second time to commit suicide five months after the birth of her daughter Julie. Mrs. Schoolar received every known form of treatment and shortly after the second infant's birth a leucotomy was performed on her.

Mrs. Schoolar has been interviewed on several occasions by the Guardian ad litem, as she seemed in some doubt as to whether she wished the Adoption to go through. She has, however, consulted Dr. Rose of Mapperley Hospital, and now feels that adoption by the applicants of this infant is in the child's best interests. Although she is in an improved state of health, she is not yet fit enough to have the care of another young child.

The infant's father has also been seen, and the effect of an Adoption Order was fully explained to him. He has given his consent to the adoption freely, as he feels that his wife is unfit to care for a second child.

This report states that our mother was adopted at eleven years of age. However, the date of her adoption order was February 21, 1945, when she would have been thirteen years and six months old. Could she possibly have lived with the Freemans from the age of eleven? If so, the guardian ad litem's report pertaining to her adoption does not mention it, merely stating that she had spent some holidays with the Freemans.

It appears she ran away from home at fifteen years of age and joined her sister Joan in lodgings at Portland House, Portland Street, Nottingham. This was a hostel for destitute women and girls.

The leucotomy took place very shortly after Jill's birth.

The social worker spent much more time speaking with me than with Jill on this occasion, which made me feel rather guilty. I think they could sense that really, I was the one still grappling with unresolved issues. Happily, Jill's adoption had been very successful, Jack and Margaret proving to be excellent parents to both Jill and her adopted sister Rosemary, who is around two and a half years older than Jill.

In the course of our discussion, I showed the social worker a letter I had sent to the attorney general, treasury solicitor, charity commission, and Notts County Council around six months earlier. It was dated December 16, 2002, and read as follows:

Dear Sirs

I am compiling a book on my family history and have been doing research in connection with this for the past 18 months. My mother, two aunts and an uncle were brought up in a privately run charitable institution called the Children's Homes, Beeston, which was situated on Imperial Road, Beeston, Nottingham, after the death of their mother from tuberculosis in 1933.

In 1947, the institution, which had opened in the 1880s, was "gifted" to the Notts Corporation by the two remaining trustees. I have accessed information regarding this at the Nottingham Archives on Canal Street, Nottingham. As this institution played such a large part in the lives of my family, it will naturally play a big part in the book I intend to write and hopefully have published.

Naturally, I wish my research to be thorough in order that I may give an accurate account of events. However, from carefully perusing this file I feel somewhat perturbed because it would appear that the handover of the Children's Homes as a gift to the Nottingham Corporation was totally illegal, in the opinion of three separate barristers. The matter was further complicated by a very generous bequest left to the Institution just 10 days after the Trustees and the over Notts Corporation signed an agreement to hand the Homes over. I have made brief notes on the contents of this file and enclose them for your information.

> *The file at the Nottingham Archives ends very abruptly leaving several serious questions unanswered. Unless I find further information, and in particular to the first two questions, I frankly cannot relate the contents of this file without it all sounding very incriminating indeed.*
>
> *I am therefore sending this letter to the offices of the Attorney General, the Treasury Solicitor, the Charity Commission and the Legal Department of Notts County Council, all of whom became involved in this matter, as you will see from the attached notes. No doubt they will have further information in their archives which explains how this matter was, presumably, resolved in a legal and ethical manner.*
>
> *I await your comments...*

Over the coming months, I received two replies from the attorney general's office and three from the Charity Commission and supplied them with as much information as I could in relation to the Children's Homes at Beeston. However, in time both of them replied to say that they could not help me due to being unable to locate any files pertaining to the matter. In a letter dated January 17, 2003, an employee with specific responsibility for advising the attorney general in relation to charity matters, replied:-

"I have searched our records and can find no mention of any file relating to this matter. This does not surprise me: files at this Office are kept only for limited periods of time, and I expect that this one was destroyed long ago."

The same employee wrote again on March 7, 2003, this time stating:

> *"You can take my earlier reply, and this one, as being on behalf of this Office and the Treasury Solicitor...I really cannot be of any more assistance."*

The Charity Commission wrote their third and final letter on March 17, 2003, in which they stated:-

> *"The current system of registration for charities was only introduced by the Charities Act 1960 but a check of the earliest records that we still hold reveals no reference under*

> any of the following names: Children's Homes Beeston; Nottingham Day Nursery and Orphanage, Imperial Road Day Nursery and Orphanage; Trust Property at Imperial Road Beeston, Mrs. M. E. Littlewood Deceased...Our records do still include some that were transferred from the Ministry of Education when the jurisdiction for educational charities passed from that Ministry to the Charity Commission in 1974. None, however, relates to this charity. In the circumstances I regret to say that we are unable to assist you any further."

I supplied Nottingham County Council with copies of all correspondence that passed between the attorney general's office, treasury solicitor, the Charity Commission, and myself. However, five months later, they still had not responded to my original letter or any of this follow-up correspondence.

The social worker could understand how this might appear highly suspicious to me but said that they were quite sure that the letters were sitting in an In-tray somewhere with nobody quite sure how to deal with them. The pressure of work everyone was under would ensure that they kept getting pushed to the bottom of the pile.

However, in the opinion of the social worker, I had a right to a reply, if only one along the lines which the attorney general's office and Charity Commission had given me. They suggested I write again, this time making it clear that a reply was expected within a certain length of time. I therefore resolved to try one more time and sent the following letter dated June 2, 2003.

> Dear Sirs
>
> I refer to my letter dated 16 December 2002, a copy of which is attached. The identical letter was also sent to the Attorney General, the Treasury Solicitor and the Charity Commission.
>
> Whilst I have received replies on behalf of the Attorney General, the Treasury Solicitor and the Charity Commission, I have not had the Courtesy of a reply from the Notts County Council. I consider this completely unacceptable.
>
> I will not reiterate the subject matter of the letters here, as I have already fully stated my concerns in further correspondence with

> *the Attorney General and Charity Commission and have always forwarded a copy of all these letters to the Notts County Council. I now attach copies of all the correspondence which has passed between myself, the Attorney General's Office and the Charity Commission.*
>
> *I repeat, I find your failure to make any response in this matter completely unacceptable.*
>
> *I will await a reply from you for the next 28 days, failing which I consider it would be reasonable for me to initiate the Notts County Council's formal complaints procedure.*
>
> *Yours faithfully,*

It really seemed to me that it would be in everyone's best interests now to bring this information out into the open, as failure to do so could only lead to the conclusion that the matter was not finally settled in a legal and ethical way, and that there was some kind of "cover-up." The dearth of any information about the Homes in local history books, libraries, and civic societies surprised and puzzled me. Although I didn't want to get hooked up on the idea of a "conspiracy theory," it really did seem that somebody/bodies wanted the existence of the Children's Homes, Beeston, wiped out of the public consciousness. The extent to which they had succeeded was impressive, considering that it operated for well over sixty years and was home to so many children.

This time I did receive a reply from the Notts County Council, and it was signed by David Spicer, assistant head of Legal Services. This was somewhat encouraging, as I knew that he had initiated the formation of the Child Migrants' Trust after Margaret Humphreys, a Nottingham social worker, had uncovered the scandal of children in care being shipped abroad to countries like Australia without the knowledge or consent of their parent/s, often to experience a life of hardship and abuse. David Spicer had personally accompanied Margaret Humphreys on one of her earliest visits to Australia to try to trace former child migrants with a view to reuniting them with their families and became a Trustee of the charity.

In her book **Empty Cradles**, Margaret Humphreys had commented that David Spicer's "sense of injustice is strong." I hoped for my sake that was still the case. In any event, I felt sure that he would at least understand the issues involved and why it was so important to me to know the facts about my mother's life and reasons for her adoption, however painful.

I arranged to visit David Spicer at his office on July 4, 2003. He listened with interest and asked appropriate questions. A young research assistant sat in and made some notes. Mr. Spicer naturally had limited resources to commit to this matter and acknowledged that it may be a difficult task to search out papers as old as these. However, I sensed that he sincerely wanted to help me if at all possible, and after taking my leave of his offices that Friday afternoon, there was a spring in my step as I crossed Trent Bridge, despite the fact that my mother had chosen this spot eighteen years earlier to escape her misery.

David Spicer sent me a letter dated July 10, 2003, in which he stated, "I will see if we can make some progress in this interesting case and let you know how we get on."

However, the months slipped by and still I heard nothing.

Finally, on November 20, 2003, I wrote to Mr. Spicer.

The letter read, in part:

> *I believe that you were completely genuine in your desire and intention to assist me in this matter. However, now that almost 5 months have elapsed since our meeting, with no apparent progress having been made, I have to ask whether any information in addition to what I already know is likely to be forthcoming?*

David Spicer suggested that we should pay a visit to the Nottingham Archives together. On January 2, 2004, I was met at the Nottingham Archives by David Spicer, who had arranged for us to have a meeting with the head archivist. As a result of that meeting, I acquired some photocopies of newspaper cuttings, which reported the official handover ceremony of the Homes to the Nottingham Corporation in July 1947. I was also informed that it was actually the city council, not the county council, who took over ownership of the Homes.

Following this meeting, David Spicer gave me the name of someone to contact at the Nottingham City Council, and I did write to them, but no new information has been forthcoming.

Perhaps it will never be known how the legal problems arising after the takeover of the Beeston Children's Homes were finally resolved or who ultimately benefited from Mary Elizabeth Littlewood's generous bequest. I would very much have liked to unearth this information, as I believe it would give me some insight into the true nature of George Thornton-Simpson. This gentleman has exercised tremendous influence in my family's lives, firstly by taking my uncle John Green under his wing at fourteen years of age and getting him started on a career in the legal profession, and later almost single-handedly, it would appear, arranging my mother's adoption by the Freemans.

However, in the absence of any official information, we shall all have to draw our own conclusions.

When I started my search, I could not possibly have imagined I would find out as much as I have, and even now I believe more information may surface in the future as archived files still in a closure period are opened to the public. As I have experienced, information sometimes comes from the most unlikely sources.

"There is nothing hidden that will not become manifest, neither anything carefully concealed that will never become known and never come into the open" (Luke 8:17).

CHAPTER 16
Fifteen Years Later

IN CHAPTER 1 OF THIS book, I recount receiving a letter in 2001 from Aunt Joan, asking for my help in finding her youngest sister, my mother. I then posed the question:-

> *"In retrospect, if I had known the emotional roller-coaster ride which awaited me, the disillusionment with myself, with others, and with the establishment, and how the strength of my relationships with family and friends would be put to the test, would I have torn the letter up and got on with my life?"*

It was too early back then to answer that question. Fifteen years later, I will attempt to answer it. However, life is a journey, and in another fifteen years I may once again feel entirely differently.

Disillusionment with myself and with others...

When I found out the facts about my mother's tragic childhood, I felt great sadness and wished I hadn't pushed her out of my life. In my defense, I have to say that, as recorded in chapter 2, I was only five when my mother left the family home after having an almighty row with my father whilst I was present in the room, which left me totally traumatized. The very next day, my father took me to live with my paternal grandparents, and it was some time before I saw my mother again.

My father's parents and his seven siblings (six sisters and one brother) were all naturally on my father's side. Hence, I never heard a good word spoken about my mother whilst I was growing up—although my grandmother always made it a policy not to speak ill of her either. This obviously influenced my feelings toward her.

My mother didn't help the situation as she seemed incapable of keeping to any regular visitation arrangements, so months would go by without my seeing her. When she did turn up, it was always completely unexpected, and I found this very emotionally distressing.

I had to reach middle age to fully appreciate the importance of the mother-daughter relationship and that possibly any kind of relationship with my mother would have been better than none at all. By then it was already too late to make up for lost time, as unbeknown to me, she took her own life in 1985 when I was thirty years of age.

It's undeniable that my birth mother abandoned me just after my fifth birthday, but I now know she was not the uncaring person I imagined from my childhood but rather a victim of events, circumstances, and attitudes over which she had no control. Her regimented upbringing in the Beeston Children's Homes and late, unsuccessful adoption by the Freemans left her ill-prepared to cope with marriage and the arrival of children and the necessary understanding and support she needed was just not available at that time. I now feel that my father also abandoned me in a sense by choosing to marry Eileen, a woman who had no intention of including me in their family life.

Incidentally, after reading this book, my step-sister Ellen emailed me to say that for some reason, her mother Eileen had always been "a very bitter woman", who "had never had a kind word to say to her grandchildren."

My grandmother, who took me in despite being old and worn out from having raised eight children of her own, was a kindly soul who had my best interests at heart. By the time she died in 1977, she had 24 grandchildren and 14 great grandchildren.

Another advantage of living with my grandmother, although I didn't realize it until many years later, was that it helped me to develop a spiritual side to my life. My grandmother wasn't a religious person. She didn't attend church although I know she believed in God. However, for a number of years whilst I was growing up, she had weekly Bible lessons with Jehovah's witnesses. I only saw these two ladies occasionally, during the school holidays, but I was always drawn to their message and to the Bible, on which the witnesses base their beliefs.

In my early teens, I asked if I could have my own Bible study, and this was arranged with the daughter of one of the ladies, who was about six years older than me. For some time, I was torn between embracing the strict moral code which the witnesses follow, or going the way of my peers at school, who were beginning to date boys and generally have greater freedoms. I even stopped my Bible study at one point, but I soon resumed it because I knew that what I was learning was the truth. I made my decision to be baptized as one of Jehovah's witnesses in 1968 at fourteen years of age, and I have never regretted it.

Disillusionment with the establishment...

Fifteen years have now passed since this book was first published under the title *In Search of a Mother*. In what was the final chapter, "Moving On," I related how, with my husband's encouragement, I had brought my search to an end and was not letting my grief over the loss of a relationship with my mother and how and why this had happened dominate my life so much.

Nevertheless, the desire to learn more about her was always in the back of my mind. I knew there were committee meeting minutes relating to the Beeston Children's Homes at the Nottingham Archives, which were due to come out of a closure period in 2016. I therefore renewed my reader's ticket in order to be able to access these records. However, I was informed by the staff that they were engaged in a project to close files which were formerly open to the public and to extend the closure period on some other files to comply with the Data Protection Act.

Consequently, the file I had waited thirteen years to be able to read for myself will now remain in a closure period for another twenty-five years, so I will be in my eighties before I am able to access it, if I am still alive by then, or even more unlikely, compos mentis! Even school admittance records, from which I was able to check the dates when my mother and her older siblings went to live at the Beeston Children's Homes and were enrolled in local schools, have now had a hundred-year closure period imposed upon them. The task of individuals trying to research their family history is therefore likely to be much more difficult in future.

About eighteen months ago, I was contacted on behalf of an elderly woman who was trying to find her long lost younger brother. He had been adopted from the Beeston Children's Homes at two years of age in 1945, the same year as my mother. She had approached Nottingham Social Services for their help in tracing him. However, she was encountering exactly the same obstacles I met with. She was told that they had no idea where his file was and that it may no longer exist. I couldn't believe that, after all the difficulties I had experienced as outlined in chapter 8, desperate people were still being fobbed off like this!

I was able to inform her that the files of adoptions from the Beeston Children's Homes were kept at the County Court on Canal Street. She in turn informed Social Services who then found her brother's file but, when I last spoke to her, had not succeeded in locating her brother.

Relationships with family and friends put to the test...

Whilst Aunt Joan was acting within the law to achieve her stated aim of having my sister and me, as Audrey's daughters, receive a third of Dorothy's inheritance, I supported her whole-heartedly. However, she had now been informed by a barrister, in no uncertain terms, that she had come to the end of the line in regard to trying to resolve the dispute with her brother John legally, and she was advised not to take the matter to court. Her solicitor acknowledged, "I know that this is a difficult thing for you to do but feel that it is really the only option as you are unlikely to receive any benefit from any proceedings and in fact quite the reverse."

I felt a sense of relief and hoped that Joan would now drop the matter. However, as recorded in chapter 15, she insisted on making a trip down to the Cotswolds to confront her brother John and later to London to try to confront her nephew at the legal firm where he practiced, getting herself arrested in the process. Surely now she had "lanced the boil," to use her own expression, she would finally settle down, perhaps even making time to get to know her nieces and our families better. It was not to be.

Joan requested that I find out the private addresses of her brother John's son, a barrister and his daughter, who was a doctor. I refused, because despite her assurances to the contrary, I knew she would be up to no good. Joan therefore obtained the addresses from a private detective and, unbeknown to me, started to barrage her nephew and niece with "derogatory" cards and letters, also sending open postcards to their places of work. This apparently went on for months. Her hate mail campaign seemed to have little impact on John's son. However, his daughter found it all very distressing.

The first thing I knew about it was when I had a telephone call from the Cheltenham Police. Apparently, my cousin, John's daughter, had made a formal complaint of harassment. Perhaps the police found it hard to accept that a woman in her eighties would do such a thing without encouragement from a younger accomplice, so they contacted me first. I assured them I had no knowledge of what Joan was doing and certainly didn't condone it although I explained to them the strength of feeling losing the legal dispute over the will had engendered in Joan.

I think the policeman who spoke to me thought I would telephone Joan immediately and warn her that a formal complaint of harassment had been made and that this would stop her in her tracks. However, I knew Joan and he didn't. I decided not to alert her because I knew that hearing that her actions were having an impact would make her even more determined to carry on. In any case, she did learn about it soon enough when a local policewoman visited her and gave her a verbal warning, which she chose to ignore. Two police officers from Cheltenham later travelled to Wales to interview her at a local police station. One rang me afterwards to tell me that they had cautioned her, and he felt sure she would now stop the harassment. Sadly, I knew better, and the matter ended up in court.

Joan appeared at Dolgellau Magistrates court in October 2005. She pleaded guilty to harassment and received a fine of £250 plus £55 costs. A restraining order was also imposed, prohibiting Joan from corresponding with the doctor (her niece, John's daughter) or turning up at her surgery. The proceedings were recorded in the *North Wales Daily Post*, along with Joan's parting comment, "I am not going to comply with the restraining order and the court can do what they like with me."

Between October 2005 and February 2007, Joan appeared in court around six times but adamantly refused to pay any fines, saying that she would "rather go to prison." One time she even took a bag packed ready in the expectation that she would be sent straight to prison after the hearing. This put the courts in a very difficult position, as she was now in her eighties. In the end, Joan was told that the court had decided to waive the fines and costs, which had by this time amounted to £675. Her "punishment" was to be held for six and a half hours whilst court proceedings continued, during which time she was brought cups of tea by a court usher. She was then discharged and faced no further punishment.

During this time, Joan became a local celebrity. Journalists were present at each court appearance, which was then reported in the local newspapers, and Joan was painted in rather a favourable light, as wanting to do the best for her nieces who had missed out on an inheritance through no fault of their own. However, I had by this time begun to have serious doubts as to Joan's real motives for getting in contact with me in the first place.

Joan never forgave me for not informing her immediately that the police had contacted me over her harassment campaign. I asked her whether she would have stopped sending the malicious cards if I had warned her. She said she wouldn't have stopped, but she would have been more prepared when the police did contact her. My "punishment" was soon to follow.

For the previous five years since she first got in touch, Joan had always phoned both Jill and me once a week for long telephone conversations, but now she decided that there was really no need to phone both of us. In future, she informed me, she would just phone Jill and she could act as the intermediary, passing any news about Joan onto me and vice versa. I wasn't at all happy about this, but Joan had made her mind up and there was nothing I could do about it. I felt resentful, though, because I had been far more proactive than Jill in assisting Joan in the early years.

Now that Joan was getting older, she had less stamina to embark on any more campaigns, so she channeled her restless energy into revising her will on a regular basis. She must have changed her will at least ten times to my knowledge. People who had been beneficiaries were taken out of it; others replaced them, often people she had known for a relatively short period of time. I felt she was using the money she had inherited from Dorothy as a means to buy friends and control people.

Jill once told me that Joan had remade her will yet again, and I remarked that I was surprised I was still in it. At this, Jill confessed that Joan was considering taking me out of her will. This really upset me because it confirmed what I had suspected for some time, that Joan was never really interested in me or Jill and our families. We had just been pawns in the power game she was playing to try to force her brother John to bend to her will.

Joan and John each inherited £180,000. Joan had said all along that, whether our deceased mother had been adopted or not, her daughters were entitled to a third share of Dorothy's estate, which would have amounted to to £60,000 each. She was prepared to give us £30,000 each of her inheritance but only, it seems, if her brother matched it. When he refused to co-operate, she gave us £10,000 each instead, saying we would get the further £20,000 and more in her will. Now she was talking about leaving me out of the will altogether!

I had been thrilled when Joan first contacted me, writing that her reason for wanting to find me was "no bad news, but would be good news for you and yours." The money wasn't the primary thing. Being able to find out the facts about my mother and her tragic childhood was more important to me.

I liked Joan initially. I regarded her as a lovable eccentric and looked forward to getting to know her better. I felt that to some extent she would make up for the mother I'd lost, but I now know that there is a darker side to her.

When I heard from Jill that Joan was thinking of taking me out of her will, childhood memories of suffering rejection flooded back. I didn't want to suffer the rejection of being written out of her will, but neither was I prepared to be like the proverbial donkey who keeps slavishly following the carrot which is dangled in front of its nose.

I therefore wrote to Joan telling her that, as she was contemplating remaking her will yet again, this was a good opportunity to ask her to leave me out of it.

On the subject of deaths, when we first got to know Joan, she told us that she was an atheist, an anti-royalist, and believed passionately in euthanasia. She would die at her own hands, she proudly assured us. She knew exactly how to go about it. It seems ironic therefore, that Joan, who was born in 1925, has outlived her three younger siblings.

Mary Gladys Green, our mother, was the first to die in 1985 at fifty- three years of age. Cause of death: suicide by drowning.

Dorothy Olive Green, our aunt, died in 1999 at seventy-two years of age. Cause of death: cancer.

John Edwin Green, our uncle, died in 2006 aged seventy-nine years of age. Cause of death: cancer.

I sincerely hope that when Joan dies it will be in her sleep, tucked up in bed in her own home. Due to my mother's suicide, I know from personal experience how awful it is to live with the knowledge that a member of your family deliberately ended their own life and you were unable to do anything to prevent it.

So, going back to the question raised in chapter 1 and at the beginning of this chapter, in retrospect...should I have torn up Joan's letter and got on with my life?

It has certainly been an emotional roller-coaster ride, and I would answer "yes," but for two things.

Firstly, I think it has been important for me to know the details of my mother's early life and why she was unable to be a mother to her own children, especially as I hope to resume our relationship in happier circumstances when the "resurrection of the righteous and the unrighteous" as spoken of in the Bible at Acts 24:15 takes place.

Secondly, in October 2013, I received an email which informed me that I have a younger sister, Denise, whom I knew nothing about. It read as follows:

> *Dear Julie,*
>
> *I am currently doing some research to find family members on behalf of my partner, Denise. Tonight, I just happened to find your book advertised via a Google search. I am attempting to connect a number of clues from a variety of sources because she was fostered under the age of two years. Denise was born in Nottingham in 1964.*
>
> *Social Services informed her she had two older sisters, one of which was adopted by another family, and that her mother's married name was Lilian Audrey Schoolar...*
>
> *Denise's mother suffered severe depression. In 1964 she had no fixed abode and moved around the Woodborough Road area of Nottingham. Subsequently Denise, who still lives in Nottingham, was placed with a foster family when social services intervened. Denise doesn't have the name of her father on her birth certificate...*

Do you think there is any connection with your family, or is it pure coincidence that you originate from Nottingham and that you are the same age as Denise's older half-sister as described by Social Services?

If you could shed any light on this mystery, we would be very grateful. You can contact me on mobile if you wish or by e-mail.

-David

When I first saw a photograph of Denise and later met her in person, I had no doubt whatsoever that she really was my sister because she resembles our mother far more closely than either me or Jill. She is petite, just like our mother, with the same swarthy skin and facial features.

Denise has no recollection of our mother but, after reading the first edition of this book (which does not contain this final chapter), can now understand the reasons why she had to be taken into long-term foster care. Her foster parents had some children of their own and a foster child whom they had already adopted. They considered adopting Denise, but our mother had refused to sign anything when social workers took her away and later relocated to another area, so they were presumably unable to contact her to obtain her consent.

I feel an affinity to Denise because, although her foster parents were loving carers, she has struggled with the same feelings of not quite belonging, or fitting in which I describe in chapter 3, when I say of being sent to live with my grandparents, "I always felt like a spare piece of furniture in their house, too good to throw out but nonetheless surplus to requirements, a bit in the way."

So, Mary Green's story is a sad tale, and I have been unable to tie up all the loose ends, which frustrates me. However, at least I have been able to tell her story, put her side of things for the first time, and I feel good about that.

In early October 2016, my husband Steve and I celebrated our forty- fifth wedding anniversary. I married very young because I was longing to have a home and a family of my own. It could easily have ended in divorce, as so many marriages do these days, but our shared faith has helped us to stay together and keep working at our relationship.

I continue to be guided and comforted by the timeless words of assurance preserved in the Bible, such as the following:

Even if my own father and mother abandon me, Jehovah himself will take me in" (Psalm 27:10).

"For the way man sees is not the way God sees, because mere man sees what appears to the eyes, but Jehovah sees into the heart" (1 Samuel 16:7b).

"Let your way of life be free of the love of money, while you are content with the present things. For he has said: 'I will never leave you, and I will never abandon you'" (Hebrews 13:5).

"He will wipe out every tear from their eyes, and death will be no more, neither will mourning nor outcry nor pain be anymore. The former things have passed away" (Revelation 21:4).

THE END

www.ingramcontent.com/pod-product-compliance
Lightning Source LLC
LaVergne TN
LVHW040150080526
838202LV00042B/3097